First Spritz Is Free

Confessions of Venice Addicts

D1403399

Edited by Kathleen Ann González

Ca' Specchio
San Jose
2018

Kathleen Ann González, 1965 –

First Spritz Is Free: Confessions of Venice Addicts

kathleenanngonzalez.com
Cover by Iris Loredana, with photos by Iris Loredana and Kate Townsend
Book Design by RJ Wofford II
ISBN: 978-1724304735
First Print Edition

"VENICE

It is a great pleasure to write the word; but I am not sure there is not a certain impudence in pretending to add anything to it. Venice has been painted and described many thousands of times, and of all the cities of the world is the easiest to visit without going there. Open the first book and you will find a rhapsody about it; step into the first picture-dealer's and you will find three or four high-coloured "views" of it. There is notoriously nothing more to be said on the subject. Every one has been there, and every one has brought back a collection of photographs. There is as little mystery about the Grand Canal as about our local thoroughfare, and the name of St. Mark is as familiar as the postman's ring. It is not forbidden, however, to speak of familiar things, and I hold that for the true Venice-lover Venice is always in order. There is nothing new to be said about her certainly, but the old is better than any novelty. It would be a sad day indeed when there should be something new to say. I write these lines with the full consciousness of having no information whatever to offer. I do not pretend to enlighten the reader; I pretend only to give a fillip to his memory; and I hold any writer sufficiently justified who is himself in love with his theme."

--Henry James, *Italian Hours*

Table of Contents

Introduction

The first time I sipped a spritz—that very Venetian drink of wine or Prosecco, Aperol or Campari, and soda water, I was repelled by its bitterness. I thought, "People *like* this?" But I found myself wanting another sip. And another. And soon the glass was empty. And then it was time for a second drink. That first spritz was free, and that wily barista knew what he was doing. I'm addicted, like many others, and have to keep going back for more.

Venice is my drug of choice. All it took was a nose full of the salt air, an eyeball full of sunlight bouncing off the water, an espresso followed by tiramisu on my tongue, stumbling down alleys into dead end canals, and I was hooked. I knew I needed to spend a chunk of my life in Venice, with a knowing I had never felt in any other city, even places I had spent considerable amounts of time, like Berlin or Vienna. Venice was different. It felt like an addiction I couldn't resist, a visceral need that pulled me back again. Whether I had the time or money to return, I had to find a way.

Turns out I'm not the only one to feel this.

We're Venetophiles, what Judith Martin (also known as Miss Manners) defines as those who love Venice—a word that mashes up the Northern Italy Veneto region and the Greek root "*philein*" meaning "to love." The contributors to *First Spritz Is Free* come from many countries, and they're also Venetians born in the city or returning after years away. In this volume, we try to describe our love for this improbable city: we've been struck by "*colpo di fulmine*," lightning love, or had love creep upon us slowly; we've been baffled or dazzled or humbled by this love; we've had families instill their love of Venice into us; and we've hung our memories on the city, like photographs clipped onto a clothesline. We put words on paper or babble over drinks as we try to make sense of this emotion we weirdly attach to a city. We don't always understand this love ourselves, but we hope that this collection of stories might provide enough puzzle pieces that you can glean the whole picture from the parts.

I first fell in love with Venice in 1996, as you'll later read about in my chapter. Since I can't be in Venice all the time, I've found ways to be there in my head instead. This has led me to read at least a hundred books about Venice and her people, to write four books myself, to pen over five hundred blog posts, and to develop a cohort of Venetophiles who commiserate with my addiction. They are novelists, bloggers, artists, musicians; they are gondoliers, tour guides, professors, and photographers. They are Venetians or travelers or ex-pats, living in their home countries or making a new home elsewhere. When I reached out to them to see if they wanted to contribute a chapter to this book, I received a thunderous, enthusiastic, and delighted reception. Some contributors introduced me to Venetophiles I didn't know, and my community grew. In fact, even more people support this project but weren't able to contribute at this time. But we all share this common love for the same city and apparently needed an outlet in *First Spritz Is Free* to share it with others. As Henry James so eloquently said, for those who are in love with Venice, there will never be enough words to describe her.

Enjoy this free book. Share it with others. All contributors wrote their chapters and shared them here for their love of the subject, without remuneration. But if you love Venice or wish to show your appreciation for it or for this project, please consider supporting one of the organizations that is dearest to us. Since 1971, the American organization Save Venice, Inc., has restored and protected Venice's architectural and artistic treasures from the ravages of weather, pollution, tourism, and time and also strives to educate people about Venice's unique patrimony. Venice in Peril, based in Great Britain, has spent over forty years saving artworks and buildings as well as conducting research into the things that threaten Venice's architectural and cultural heritage. More recently, the creative grassroots group Comitato No Grandi Navi is raising awareness, calling for sustainable tourism practices, and preventing large cruise ships from wreaking further damage to the architecture, Venetian culture, and the very lagoon itself. Supporting these groups helps Venice live on as a thriving culture and city for future generations so that others can visit this unique place and become addicted to it as well.

Here I offer you these tastes of Venice to give you your fix or to get you hooked. Though the first sip of your spritz may be a bitter one, these chapters are filled with sweetness and leave you wanting more. Go grab your drink of choice, sit back, and enjoy!

"Three Small Stories" by Piero Bellini

My first goal has always been to not leave the lagoon. At the end of high school (Liceo Classico "Marco Polo," difficult to imagine something more Venetian...) when I had to choose which University to enroll in, I almost automatically applied to Ca' Foscari, *Economia e Commercio*, here in Venice, avoiding Medicine, Law, Engineering etc., ... for which I would have had to go to the nearby town of Padua. At the end of my university studies in 1984, I had received interesting job offers, for example at Fiat in Turin, but I preferred more simply to be content with a job at the local Cassa di Risparmio (savings bank), and not to detach myself from my beloved city. When I was looking for a house, it would have been easier and cheaper to move to Mestre, on the "mainland," though still the City of Venice. With my wife Lorenza we preferred to initially live in a smaller house that needed to be restored, but in the historic center. Lorenza, in fact, thinks like me. She is also Venetian and so, too, logically, our son Oscar. My deeply Venetian choice may seem very conservative. Actually I love traveling, also because I know where I want to come back to: here to my lagoon! And anyway there is the whole world (lately becoming more exaggerated!) that comes to visit us.

I have a thousand reasons to explain my love for my city, but I would run the risk of falling perhaps into trivialities. I prefer to tell you three little stories about the Hotel Bisanzio, a few steps from Piazza San Marco, in Calle della Pietà, where Antonio Vivaldi in the eighteenth century directed his famous choir of "*putte*." The hotel, a past investment of my grandfather Fiorenzo, has belonged to the family (uncles and cousins) for many decades.

Hotel Bisanzio Episode 1: "Destiny"

In 1974 with my parents Edda and Toto and my sister Stella, we decided to spend a few days of vacation in Paris (also a city that I love). We took the opportunity to greet some friends, the Germann family, who at that time lived in a splendid, classic Parisian house on Place Jussieu. In those days they had a guest, a nice American boy, Tom. When he heard that we were from Venice, he seemed surprised and told us that for many years his uncle and aunt in New York, Bob and Jeanne, had the habit of going on holiday to my city: he would certainly talk to them about us. At the time obviously there were no emails, cell phones, Facebook, etc. ... So we gave to Tom, because it related to his uncle and aunt, a slip of paper with our name, surname, home phone number, and address: Castello 3597. Who knew that, among the many quirks of Venice, there are the house numbers? Venice is divided into *sestieri*: Castello, San Marco, Dorsoduro, San Polo, Santa Croce, Cannaregio. Each of these includes thousands of house numbers. Often tourists stop us on the street asking for directions like "Please ... Cannaregio 2462?" We Venetians extend our arms and shake our heads. Even if they ask for the name of a *calle*, often the result is the same: there are many *calli* with the same name! Easier if we talk about a *campo*; but there too there may be problems (for example, Campo San Stin, Campo Sant'Agostin).

Returning to our story, back in the USA Tom gave our paper to his uncle and aunt who in a few months would leave for their usual vacation in Venice. Destiny was doing his job.... The hotel where Tom's uncle and aunt were customers for years was, unbelievably, the Hotel Bisanzio! Bob and Jeanne, arriving in Venice, like always were greeted by my uncle Primo. "Mr. and Mrs. Blank, welcome back to Venice!" "Hi, Mr. Primo, nice to see you again. Could you please do us a little favor? Where is it this address Castello 3597?"

With huge surprise my uncle said, "But ... but ... this is my address!!??"

In fact he lives on the third floor of the building and my parents on the second! In this very particular way a great friendship was born between two families that still lasts through the generations, even if Jeanne and my father have not been with us for a while and also Bob has left us recently at the venerable age of 102 years!

This extraordinary series of coincidences has shown me three things:

1) Venice is special, 2) the world is small, 3) God exists.

Hotel Bisanzio Episode 2: "First Working Day"

As it happens to many young university students, in 1978-79 my pockets were rather empty! So I tried to flesh out the poor wallet thanks to a variety of occasional jobs, often interesting, very interesting ones! Guardroom at the famous Biennale of Contemporary Art in the gardens of Castello. "*Scattino*" in restaurants: I took souvenir pictures of tourists at the time of the appetizer, and I managed to bring them back with a book of matches attached to the back and a picture of the bell tower of San Marco when they were concentrating on dessert. No digital, no laser printer: the photos were at that time developed by a friend in a small, traditional darkroom ... a real fight against time. I often arrived at the restaurant with freshly dried pictures, and the tourists had already left! But I remember that period with warmth and fun, however. The most beautiful occasional work was certainly that of appearing in some works at the Fenice Theatre—a fantastic experience that I would recommend to anyone!

Among my occasional activities, one of the most significant was that of (substitute) night porter, of course at the Hotel Bisanzio. Mauro, the official night employee, was entitled to his "day" (or night?) of rest, so I gave up my Saturday night with friends to put myself, dark jacket and tie, behind the counter of this beautiful hotel. Today Venice is always invaded by masses of tourists, but at that time the hotels in the historic center were perhaps a twentieth of what we have today, and January was very low season: a few brave tourists walked through the cold, damp, and semi-deserted *calli* of the city. My work started on a frozen Saturday night, lashed by rain and wind, at the beginning of January. My Uncle Primo explained the work to me and told me not to worry: the occupied rooms were only three or four out of a total of forty. Given the bad weather that raged, certainly we were not waiting for any other evening arrivals. I was a bit excited and aware of having alone on my shoulders throughout the night the management of an important 4-star hotel: not easy for a twenty-year-old guy without the slightest experience in this regard.

Being my first night at work, my Uncle Primo stayed with me until about 10 p.m. Then he went home, a short five minute walk.

At the main entrance of the Hotel Bisanzio one enters through the long Calle della Pietà, which starts from the Riva degli Schiavoni, next to the church of the same name. Wind and rain increased in intensity, and nobody seemed to want to go there. At about 10:30 p.m. I found myself a bit surprised by some men in

5

uniform who were heading towards our entrance. Cold and wet, they came into the hall of the hotel.

"How can I help you, sir?" I addressed an officer accompanied by four or five American sailors in uniform.

"We need a room for tonight. Our big aircraft carrier *Nimitz* is out in the Adriatic Sea, and we cannot reach it with our boat shuttle service because of the storm. I will pay the bill with this US Navy credit card."

Not without surprise, I gave them the keys of two or three rooms. After a few minutes, another five or six sailors entered the hotel and ... same story ... another two or three rooms were taken. Incredibly, for the season, in less than an hour the Bisanzio was full! And other people from the *Nimitz*, wet and cold, were still coming in. At that point the phone rang. My Uncle Primo asked me from his house, "Hi, Piero ... is it all right? All quiet?"

"Well," I replied, "the hotel is full and I have people who keep coming inside. What should I do?"

"Are you kidding?" said Primo.

"Absolutely not, Uncle ... and if you want to see your hotel again in good shape tomorrow morning, it's better if you come back here immediately!"

So he did and could see that I was not joking at all. We had to set up officers and sailors on the sofas in the bar, on the floor of the breakfast room, and in every accessible corner of the hotel! At a certain point, thank God, the influx of men in uniform stopped. So my uncle, very tired, went home. Of course, I could not sleep a single minute that night. I only remember that in the morning the big three liter bottle of Johnny Walker whisky from the bar was absolutely empty!

But the appearance of a cold, sunny, and calm morning suggested to me that this strange nightmare was heading towards its happy ending.

Hotel Bisanzio Episode 3: "Cinema!"
My grandfather, Fiorenzo Zambon, born in 1901, came from Dardago, an ancient, small, and poor peasant village in Friuli Venezia Giulia (northeast of Venice), near the current important American military base in Aviano.

At the end of the 1920s, he decided to move with his family to Venice, in search of fortune. In the eyes of humble people, accustomed to a limited and rural life, Venice could have in fact appeared at the time as a large and rich metropolis. Despite the fact that his education had stopped at the end of elementary school, Fiorenzo was a skilled and experienced building contractor. In the years and decades in Venice, his company restored many houses and important buildings, not disdaining, if the opportunity was presented, to do some good business in the real estate market. So it was that around 1963 he decided to buy the old and battered Cinema Savona, at the bottom of the Calle della Pietà, attended especially by soldiers, sailors, and servants, with the idea of making apartments and maybe even a small *pensione*.

With the arrival of television in the Venetians' houses, the cinemas were slowly dying and, as in many other cities, they had begun to close and be replaced by supermarkets, hotels, shops, and so on; one of the most spectacular examples of these conversions is the recent restoration of Cinema Italia, in Strada Nuova, which has become one of the most striking supermarkets in the world. My grandfather was a pioneer from this point of view. And so the old cinema that was called Savoia before 1945, and later Savona (after the war, with the newly formed Italian Republic, the surname of the old King of Italy was no longer in fashion!) in the '60s became first Albergo Savona and a few years later, following other renovations, the current Hotel Bisanzio. Soon you will understand why this long introduction was necessary.

Now after a few months of work, I had fully taken possession of my role as night porter, and I was able to solve the most varied problems on the fly: arrivals of tourists late at night, early departures in the first morning, sudden toilet flushing to be repaired, satisfying impossible demands of bizarre clients, consoling young tourist girls with insomnia, diverting telephone requests from jealous husbands while the wife was having fun with the friend on duty, etc. ...

But the unexpected was always around the corner! On a relatively calm evening, I saw a staggering, elderly, and rustic Venetian man approaching the entrance. Unfortunately, I did not have time to block the opening of the doors, and I found him in front of the main desk. With a serious and decisive air I heard, "*Uno platea e un scartosso de bagigi!*" Translating from the Venetian dialect: "One ticket in the stalls and a box of peanuts, please!"

It was not easy to convince him, because of his alcohol level, that this had not been a cinema for decades, and now he was in the entrance of a 4-star hotel. After several unlucky attempts to make him move from there, I managed to solve the problem by putting in his hand two fresh bottles of beer, offered by myself, and accompanying him decisively outside the door! For a moment the Hotel Bisanzio, mindful of its glorious celluloid past, was the scene of a short neo-realist movie that would have been nice to make known to the public of the famous Mostra del Cinema di Venezia!

Biography

Piero Bellini, born in 1958 in Venezia, still living here with his wife Lorenza and their son Oscar. He works for a local saving bank now merged with the biggest Italian bank. For many years he was a dealer in the foreign exchange and money market.

Piero is the author of a funny comic book MATTAMATICA (Madmath) where the main actors are numbers and geometric shapes. More seriously he also wrote a book about British war economy and finance during the Second World War.

Piero's hobby is jazz music, and he plays piano and makes jazz compositions together with other Venetian friends. In Venice, perhaps it will be a surprise for someone, there is a quite solid jazz tradition and also a good Jazz Club. Jazz music (as well as baroque!) is often around!

9

"Venice: (More) Writing Under the Influence"
by Rita Bottoms

How prescient the dream in Notebook #31, October 2006 "I am looking down from a window on the top floor of the Palazzo and it is a surprise to see my Mother and I walking hand in hand toward Piazza San Marco   I can see the Grand Canal from one end to another and   it amazes me   that the *Fondamenta* runs along uninterrupted for the entire length of this great waterway   at the far end a spectacular fountain rises at least a hundred feet into the air its   delicate pink marble facade has columns with ornately carved acanthus leaves and must measure fifty feet across   fleshy peach figures of sea nymphs and creatures spout and splash   I am astonished for here is *La Fonte*   the Source of the Grand Canal" Venice her waters the source   my element   inspiration everywhere in mirrors   mounds of arugula and artichokes   church floors damask wallpapers   waiters and baristas   old men standing with *ombras*   women in capes and fur hats   small brown and white dogs   brocades   silk velvets   stone slabs   *Cuba Rhum pavimenti palazzzi*   floors *marmorizzata* of inks in puddles on papers   chiming of the bells on Sunday   bindings of leather vellum books   crimson red glass   gondoliers and shop keepers tossing back espresso   bridges   monkfish   mesh bags of *vongole veracci*   Home to the redheaded Muse and her Consort so receptive   inspiring and inclusive   the Publisher ever welcoming continually bringing forth and   manifesting artistically   his mother and   wife the watercolorist purveyors of beautiful books   the hand printer and teacher   the Venetian friend and art lover   the necklace maker   that small   wondrous handful   that   gathering of encouragers enliveners inspirers who welcome my wild ideas with whom I am always home

What a far cry from those fledgling days of the early '60s when I knew everything and when my girlfriend and I made   our eighteen month Grand European and Middle Eastern Tour. We had often heard that Venice had a terrible smell and so we steered clear of her. A few years later traveling from Amsterdam to Trieste, when my train made a stop for one hour at *Stazione Santa Lucia*, I figured I might as well stretch my legs and take a look. Down the steps of the *Stazione* I went and you know the rest. Stunned by the sight and vitality of the Grand Canal in the midst of the city on the water, I knew I had to return. And by myself immersed in the quiet mists of November, I wandered the city, besotted, an *incurabile*, beyond all hope. There were several other brief visits. But were it not for writer and artist, Mark Bloch's long friendship with the artist, Ray Johnson, and my connection with Ray, you would not be reading this. Ray brought us together, and it was at Mark's urging, that I applied for, and received, a writing Residency through the generosity of The Emily Harvey Foundation, which took my husband Tom and me to Venice for six weeks in 2012. Unable to stay away, we return every year.

In my notes of Norman O. Brown's Myth and History class he said "Nothing in the mind is ever forgotten but can be brought to light again under the right conditions…the mind is the Eternal City." I find my Venetian afterlife in dreams, in the water and in mirrors. I stare into a photograph of the old man reading at a lone table inside the Caffè Florian or at endless snapshots taken of the green waters of the Grand Canal looking down into it from a seat on a *vaporetto* or I obsess over the Italian names of spices *radice di genziana cumino di Malta* or *timo secco* at Drogreria Mascari and the colors of the spice ziggurats in the window or the taste of the many *Cuba Rhum caramelli* purchased there dreams continue and the mind riffs on obsessions a palette of color pigments and silk skeins on exhibition at Palazzo Mocenigo and last night I am looking through a worn sample book of damask silk very fragile pieces the book disintegrating in my hands I am speaking in dialect to merchants in an old shop I have never seen before entering Venice on the water for the first time pinch me the Grand Canal is flowing by as I shop for artichokes and zucchini in the Rialto Mercato besotted with the great waterway weeks before we go home I worry for the day we have to leave in countless photographs I try to capture its color that green the oil painter's viridian to see when I close my eyes thousands of miles away I search for old mirrors the more worn dimly lit aged and foxed the more I am magnetized by them I am drawn into their faded surfaces

11

imperfections visible   sometimes slightly broken mysteries of their construction and seeds of their dissolution revealed I look into the mirrors of Palazzo Mocenigo Caffè Florian and Querini Stampalia witnesses in boudoir and tea room and privy to intimacies endlessly reflected on their surfaces not to see my own reflection   but to dissolve into them one of their immortals

How fortunate that Venice is in our midst at home as Tom has painted a number of beautiful oils that hang in the parlor, living room, dining room and hall of our Santa Cruz home so we can look down the Rialto Bridge on *gondole* and a *motoscafo* flying out of the painting, see Ca' d'Oro and other *palazzi* across the canal from our *vaporetto* stop, Rialto Mercato, see   the   Procuratie and Caffè Florian windows with ourselves and our friends looking out of them the *maestro* at the Quadri with musicians and chairs in the great Piazza   gondolier on the lagoon   San Vio with a gondola chair sitting alongside the canal   a mountain of burgundy and white striped *tardivo* at Rialto Mercato   reflections of the dining room looking into the large mirrored wall at Ristorante Peoceto Risorto San Giorgio from Giudecca and two views of Bacino Orseolo *gondolieri* at night and early morning   living so far away how important my friendship with the painter Robert Morgan the one to whom Joseph Brodsky's Venice classic, *Watermark* is dedicated who has lived in Venice almost forever

It's an unstated assumption that I'm always coming back so I need to say that   the very narrow light red and cream striped Palazzetto Tron Memmo built in 1871 along the Grand Canal between Palazzo Corner Contarini del Cavalli and Palazzo D'Anna Martinengo Volpi di Misurata in Sestiere San Marco belongs to me although the current residents may not know this. It is visible across from the *vaporetto* stop San Silvestro as you are going in the direction of Salute. Look quickly as it is a sliver of a building. I should also mention that not so long ago I paid good money for a beautiful pink damask paper medallion trimmed with gold paper rickrack and gold paper tassels and ordered that a calligrapher write underneath "*Residente per sempre de Venezia*," which is framed and sits in my small writing room. I am amassing quite a cache of *Cuba Rhum* wrappers silver and gold foils from candies particular reds and greens from various magazines   and oyster shells   pieces of mirrors   photographs of damask   photographs of mirrors   red and blue striped paper straws   from which I   plan to make a   huge Venice piece in the form of a large leporello style screen.   I've been piling up these goods for about six years now.

In 2013   I wrote the following   One by one as my longer fingernails broke off I saved them in my pocket and threw them into the Grand Canal whether they sank or floated out into the lagoon it was my way of staying in Venice it was my way of never leaving

Biography

Rita Bottoms was Librarian and Curator of Special Collections at the University of California, Santa Cruz, and worked with many photographers, writers, musicians, publishers, artists, and filmmakers. Her books of particular interest to Venetophiles are Riffs & Ecstasies, Venice *with paintings by Tom Bottoms (Cafe Margo 2013);* Riffs & Ecstasies: True Stories, *in Italian & English* (Damocle Edizioni, *Venezia 2014); and,* Venice: Writing Under the Influence, *in Italian & English (Damocle Edizioni, Venezia 2016). These books are available at City Lights Bookstore, San Francisco; Libreria Pino, San Francisco; Bookshop Santa Cruz; Bookshop Damocle Edizioni, Venezia, and from the author at cafemargo@baymoon.com.*

"Venice, the Mirror of the Soul" by Manuel Carrión

I arrived in Venice in 2011 to attend the Venice Art Biennale. Since my arrival, it was like love at first sight. I looked around and my soul understood that destiny had brought me to this city for some particular reason.

I love Venice with all my heart, and I feel that she is like a love that helps you grow and be yourself day after day. I often say that Venice is like a mirror of the soul that reflects beautiful things, even those that we want to hide. This makes us enter into a constant dialogue with the child inside us.

I particularly chose to live at Giudecca to admire it, watch it, breathe it, and contemplate it.

Here, I found the meaning of my life, which is to be an artist. One day, on November 4, 2013, when I finished my last day of seasonal work in Hotel Ca' Nigra, walking and reflecting on my future arrival in Campo San Barnaba, I wondered, "What will I do now?" A light that came from the heart spoke to me and said, "Become the most famous artist of the twenty-first century." Since then, I have embarked on this alchemical path that led me to create a spiritual journey full of satisfactions.

Currently I am working on two projects that without Venice and its gratitude never could have existed. One of them is the Opus Magnum, a mosaic composed of art works of 65,536 people that is to be presented in the Venice Art Biennale of 2021.

The other dream I am building on is about creating a cultural and artistic district where artists dialogue to build a community in which art comes to be the center of society. This neighbourhood is located in the island of San Giorgio, Giudecca, and Sacca Fisola. I call it the Venetian Soho.

Biography

Manuel Carrión is an Ecuadorian artist, born in Quito on September 23rd, 1983. Since he was a child, he was influenced by a well-known family in the political and cultural life of the capital of Ecuador. At an early age, he has been distinguished by his sensitivity, which led him to deal with complex topics such as philosophy, and to broaden his sphere of interests to the theme of the development of human potential.

With intense work, he managed to produce countless works, which can be found in the main European capitals and around the world, mainly in Venice, Paris, New York, Kyoto, and Quito.

Facebook: m.facebook.com/manuelcarrionvenezia/
Instagram: @artist_manuelcarrion_venice
manuelcarrion.com
allaricercadel108.com

"Venice: An Addiction that Cannot Be Cured!"
by Monica Cesarato

A hot, sweltering, typical summer day in Italy in 1972.

My father's Vespa dashes fast along the Ponte della Libertà, the nearly four kilometer bridge built by Mussolini in 1933, connecting the *terraferma* to the beautiful city of Venice.

Standing upright on the footrest at the front, nestled between my father's arms while he rides, peeking on my right, I can just make out the outlines of Porto Marghera, one of the largest coastal industrial areas in Europe, so imposing with its high chimneys and towers.

To my left I can see a train whizzing by, all windows open, passengers trying to catch a breath of fresh air, disheveled hair and red faces: trains in Italy in the '70s did not come with air conditioning!

My mother is a pillion at the back, wearing a headscarf, her straying pitch-black hair locks escaping the grip of the silk cloth. My dad, so dashing with his thick moustaches, looks like a motorbike racer. None of us is wearing a safety helmet, of course!

The windshield stops the hot air and the thousands of mosquitoes from crashing into my face, and I am so thankful for that: I tasted ants and mosquitoes a few weeks back, did not like them much!

I laugh, exhilarated by the sight which appears to my eyes and the sensation of speed—in all fairness, knowing my dad, he probably was going very slow, but to me it felt like we were going as fast as a Ferrari Testarossa!

And then I can see it in all its beauty, breathtaking, standing on water, like a heron: there it is, Venice!

Summer 1972: I was only three years old, but already the city entered into my bloodstream, like a good disease, a delightful virus which would never leave me, would never be cured, no matter how far I went and how long for!

In the years to come I would cross over that bridge a thousand times, over and over: first with my uncle, in his old Fiat 500, when he took me fishing for *seppie*, Venetian cuttlefish, which we would then eat grilled on the barbeque with all the family; then on the local bus on my way to high school, the Tourism and Language Institute, where I would learn about the history and importance of Venice; and many years later, each and every time I went to the city for one of my food tours or cooking classes.

And every single time was, and is, like the first time: my eyes linger first to the right to catch glimpses of Marghera, then to my left to look at the railway line and the passing trains. And every time I see the outlines of the city looking ahead, it's like that first summer day! A grin comes naturally to my face, and I feel like I am going home. (I can't start laughing, otherwise the people on the bus will think I am crazy, but I do laugh if I am driving there on my own, so you know!)

I am not Venetian, technically speaking, as I was not born and raised in Venice itself, but on the mainland, in the countryside, only five kilometers away. Venetian people classify us as *campagnoli*, countryside people, therefore my true home is not really Venice. But to me, it is: I always felt like I belong there, like I am meant to be there.

I remember once, I was walking around with a couple of friends and I started caressing the decaying walls of a building in a small calle and it felt like I was caressing a friend.

I still live in the countryside, but I am very lucky because I get to be in Venice very often during the week, due to my work as a food guide and cooking instructor, teaching people the delights of Venetian food. But to be honest, I try to find other excuses to go into the city, if I do not have to be there for work.

There are periods when I do not have to go into the city for days on end, so I make up excuses to make my way there, even if it is only for a few hours!

I am truly addicted!

Not sure why, since most of the time the city is jam-packed with trampling tourists and horrible souvenir shops, which, in summer, believe me, coupled with the *afa*, the terrible humidity which permeates the whole city, is a huge deterrent!

But the ancient buildings, the green canals, the harsh and colorful people, their beautiful boats, the amazing Venetian food and wine: all of it is truly intoxicating.

I can never get enough of it.

Even on the days when the crowds of tourists are way too many; when for one reason or another the *vaporetti* are not running and you have to walk all across the city and more; when your clients don't turn up and they do not even bother telling you; when it rains cats and dogs and you forgot your umbrellas in some *osteria* or the fog is so thick and cold, you could cut it with a knife; when the heat is so intense you can hardly breathe and all you can do is melt away in sweat, even then I simply can't get enough of this amazing city.

I cannot get enough of hearing the old ladies chatting and gossiping away in the Venetian language, holding their bags full of the fresh fish and goodies they got at the historic Rialto Market; cannot get enough of watching the skillful gondoliers, dodging their way through the canals, swearing at each other and always looking like they are about to start a fight, when all they are doing is telling each other what they did on the weekend; cannot get enough of popping my head in the shops of my many artisan friends, stealing away some of their time in chats, while peeking at their next stunning creation; cannot get enough of going from *bàcaro* to *bàcaro*, eating the traditional *cicchetti*, sampling some new ones and being the tester/taster for the owners, asking for my opinion on a new wine or cocktail; cannot get enough of listening to my writer, poet, and historian friends, telling me about the legends and traditions of the Republic of Venice, bringing back to life the buildings, water wells, and columns which are spread all over town; cannot get enough of simply walking into the Campo de Gheto Novo and wondering how the Jews of Venice ever managed to live in such a restricted area, in such terrible conditions.

I simply cannot get enough of living Venice!

Venice: a city that you either love or hate, simple as that—and I love it!

Biography

Monica Cesarato, food and travel blogger, Venice lover, cooking instructor and food guide, but simply an overall talker—creator of #aphotoofveniceaday

Twitter: @monicacesarato.com @cookinvenice
Facebook: Monica Cesarato and Cook In Venice
Instagram: @monicacesarato,   @cookinvenice
@aphotofveniceaday

"Building a Venice of My Own" by Adriano Contini

The tale of my encounter with Venice begins in the deep South, in Bari, in the 1970s. Military service was compulsory back then, and I found myself in some dilapidated barracks 500 kilometers away from home, immersed in a colorful babel of dialects. For the most part the people there would come together on a regional and hence linguistic basis. In this chaos an anomalous, stiff figure stood out, with an English-style rider's jacket—one of those with a slit at the back. This is how I met Stefano, an old-fashioned Venetian enamored with his city. He was constantly talking about it. Released from our toilsome duties, we met again: in Rome, where I have always lived, and in Venice, his hometown. I started visiting the city several times a year, not as a tourist but as a Venetian; I was effectively under cover, in disguise and undetectable, at any rate until I opened my mouth. Over time I had learned to understand Venetian, but obviously whenever I spoke, it was easy to see that I was an outsider. Since I was not staying at a hotel, I experienced everyday life in the city: groceries at the market, aperitifs, pastimes—and the many cultural opportunities offered by the city.

In other words, I experienced the city from within—a rare privilege. The best way to explore the city was by boat. We would travel down the inner canals, gazing at the palaces from their true perspective: the canal doors. We would travel to the islands, some laden with history and colors, others deserted and abandoned for centuries, their old ruins gradually being eroded by the brackish dampness and by the fog which envelops the city and its environs in winter.

It would be pointless to try and list all the things, or even the most interesting things, I have seen in such a long period—practically most of my life. Some things stand out in my memory, like flashbacks: the excitement I felt when making my way down the meandering Torcello canal by boat for the first time and seeing the little bridge, and the old tavern with peacocks ambling about on its perfectly mowed lawn. As we sat there sipping our *ombre* (small glasses of wine), we felt words were superfluous, if not annoying. I remember the Scuola Grande di San Rocco, which on a summer evening offered the exuberance of Vivaldi's *Juditha Triumphans:*

when beauty exceeds certain boundaries, you feel at a loss. I wasn't sure whether I should focus on what I felt or what I saw, and I continued to pass from one feeling to the next, as though trying to freeze those moments and never let them go. I remember the light illuminating the large altarpiece by Bellini at San Zaccaria, with colors so vivid it was as though they had just been applied; and I remember St. Mark's on Christmas Eve, as we sat on its icy stones.

Yet there was also more to Venice, which back then had not yet become depopulated as it is today, when the inhabitants are down to one third of what they were in the eighteenth century. Venice was still alive, with its small shops and food stalls under the porticoes at Rialto. The city had not yet fallen victim to the devastation that has gutted it, turning it into a figment of its former self, a beautiful film set without any inhabitants. You could sense Venetianness at every word or step, in every *bàcaro* (wine bar), *cicchetto* (savoury snack), or glass. I immersed myself into a new and mysterious language: Prosecco and spritz, *esse buranei, bussolai, baccalà, garusoli* and *moeche, bigoli, fritole,* and countless wines with mysterious and evocative names—*raboso, clinto, fragolino, bacò,* and *malbec.* A kaleidoscope of encrypted novelties that I discovered one by one.

In order to eat and drink like a Venetian, you needed to learn the language. It was a small step from this to a sociology of Venetianness. I came to believe that some traces of the pomp of the sixteenth, seventeenth, and especially eighteenth centuries must have trickled into the present, that the traits of the inhabitants of the Most Serene Republic must somehow have passed through successive generations down to the present day. There is a saying that goes *"Veneziani gran signori"* ("Venetians great gentlemen"), meaning that the Venetians of old were tolerant men of the world open to innovation and diversity, and opposed to the cultural and especially dogmatic strictures that held a firm sway over the world in those golden centuries, leading to bloody religious wars. I imagined the Venetians as somehow different from others, as averse to ideological censorship yet at the same time faithful to the tradition and rules of good government—in other words, as unique characters. I reached the conclusion that the eighteenth century had been the moment of greatest splendor, the peak of the city's trajectory, the period concealing the greatest treasures. So I chose to find someone who could show me eighteenth-century Venice, just as

I had found some Venetians to show me the present-day one. I had always had a fascination with the history of material, everyday life, with the small things that make up people's lives. I came across a very peculiar Venetian: Giacomo Casanova, a great memorialist, perhaps the greatest of the eighteenth century—certainly the only one to have provided a socially inclusive description of such a class-conscious age, in a period in which memoir writing was an exclusive pursuit of the ruling elite, who didn't have the faintest idea of how the common folk lived. Casanova is an extremely modern memorialist because he is sincere, direct, even ruthless when it comes to his own weaknesses and those of others, even though this exposes him to the charge of cynicism (which is not unfounded). He takes us on a journey to explore this period, transporting us into this reality and bringing it to life, allowing us to experience it from within rather than without.

In my wanderings I seamlessly passed from one age to the other. The common thread linking these different ages was the language, one more suited to beau-filled salons than feats of arms. Casanova's *Iliad* in Venetian: a minuet more than a war. Then there was that spirit which had always distinguished the Venetians: a mellowness that was always witty yet civil, never over the top or coarse. The more I entered into contact with figures from the past—especially the most famous salon patronesses of that bygone age—the more I perceived its elegant spirit: its *morbìn*, as it was called by Goldoni, who entitled one of his comedies *Le morbinose* (*The Good-Humoured Ladies*). We have chronicles describing how the Venetians used to behave at the theatre, namely with a very different demeanour from the solemn and silent one to be observed in other capitals. Quips would echo through the boxes, and each word would carry others through sparkling and libertine social jousting. Some renowned noblewomen are still remembered for their witty remarks and the nonchalance and spiritedness with which they responded to bold advances.

I wasn't quite sure what remained of all this, yet I felt that something must have survived-it was as though it exuded from the very stones of the city. I started wandering and getting lost. In Venice—more of a dream world than a real place—it was quite easy for me to get lost; in fact, it still is. Could I blame the city, which looked like a maze made up of traps and narrow *calli* (alleyways)

23

leading to canals? The alternative routes I sought out in an attempt to avoid the crowds of tourists would sometimes lead me back to my starting point. I learned to put up with the idea of losing my bearings; I would walk as though in a trance, in a state in which feelings would stream through me beyond the grasp of reason. These aimless itineraries would lead me to isolated places that won my heart more than the famous landmarks: San Pietro di Castello, with its off-kilter bell tower, its church, lawn, benches, and the walls of the Arsenale—practically a deserted place; other gardens, like that of Palazzo Contarini dal Zaffo, with the perfectly preserved Casino degli Spiriti, a silent place crossed by busy nuns in flowing white robes; and San Francesco della Vigna, with its beautiful cloister unexpectedly located near a gasometer—a reminder of the times in which the city was lit by gaslights.

Over time I had come to realize that in Venice you mustn't get caught up in the obsession of having to visit all the major monuments, palaces, and churches. Because the most beautiful thing in Venice is precisely the maze of *calli*, a labyrinth offering an unexpected glimpse of a courtyard, small church, or lesser-known (yet no less interesting) palace. People always return to Venice sooner or later, so if you miss something, you can always make up for it the next time. In fact, it's better to have a reason to return to the city, some crucial landmark you haven't seen yet.

Venice is synonymous with water, as well as stone, and every part of it is best seen from the water: the best glimpses are always from a bridge, a boat, a *vaporetto* (waterbus), or an island. The San Marco waterfront, in all its dazzling majesty, is best viewed from the Giudecca, as is San Giorgio. The islands offer a wide array of vistas, as though to illustrate the various stages of development across the centuries: Torcello shows us what the lagoon must have been like when it was first settled, with its banks still reinforced by stakes, and bushes and grass almost reaching the water. With its brightly colored houses, extravagant yet beautiful, Burano reflects the kind of fishermen's settlements whose work used to replenish the Rialto Market day after day. Sant'Erasmo, the vegetable garden of Venice, offers an agricultural landscape of a sort that seems foreign to the lagoon. Murano is synonymous with the industriousness of its master glassblowers, who are both craftsmen and brilliant artists.

For me, Venice is the only place where you enjoy being alone. The city is a powerful presence that accompanies you at every step and does not leave you longing for anything else. Its stones have been smoothed down by the steps of those who have come before us across the centuries. I don't know why, but these traces here seem more visible, these men more real. Each of them, however important he may have been, must have felt like me—small by comparison to the immense beauty of the city. In Venice it is easier to accept the limits and finiteness of time. I've had the opportunity to get to know this city, and that is enough.

This, then, is the tale of my connection with Venice: a long tale that spans several decades and speaks of a life parallel to my own, a life that unfolded there, in a world apart. Many years and steps later, it is difficult for me to describe the present, because the city is becoming increasingly dispirited. Yet this is no reason to take an anachronistic approach: each age must be taken for what it is. There have been times of war, famine, pestilence, invasions, canal-filling, and the demolition of churches in which noblemen and common folk, artists and *arsenalotti*, were buried. We must therefore also put up with the devastation wrought by tourism and depopulation. We can still seek refuge in the maze of *calli*, lose our bearings, and get lost in our dreams. We can discover the excitement of entering empty churches or abandoned *squeri* (boat yards). We can visit the city outside the tourist season, by picking a time other than Carnival, the Biennale, or the film festival period. We can trade great parties and fireworks displays for silence, the loss of our bearings, and solitude. We can steer clear of the human wave that engulfs, devours, and shatters everything.

Ultimately, over time, I have built a Venice of my own, which is only partly real: it is the sum of all my journeys, days, encounters, arrivals, and departures—in the sun or rain, snow or fog. It is the Venice of my memories: a city of the soul—a secret garden to which I can always return, if not in body, at least in my mind. And I believe all those who have loved and visited Venice before me have done this, too. Venice is a generous lover who asks no questions and expects nothing of you. She gives you her colors, sounds, and scents. She is always waiting for you and never enquires when you will visit her again. Ultimately, each of us celebrates her magic and preserves her legend, and this gives her life, eternally, as though time did not exist.

Biography

Adriano Contini was born in Rome, where he still lives. After graduating from high school, he earned a Law degree at the Sapienza University of Rome. He later worked as a business consultant and statutory auditor. A lover of Venice and Casanova scholar, he firmly believes in the need to popularize studies on eighteenth-century Venice, based on an accurate and up-to-date use of the sources. Since 2004 he has been taking part in the Wikipedia project, by personally writing—or else contributing to—numerous entries on Giacomo Casanova and his milieu.

"Venetian Dreams" by Marisa Convento

I remember when I first understood Venice, it was back in the early eighties: a summer night and we were out in the lagoon aboard a friend's boat coming back from a dinner on Burano. The sky was full of stars and my nose full of the scent of fine sprays of water. I could hear seagulls chatting among themselves despite the noise of the outboard engine. That warm and humid summer night, I felt in love with my new city.

But before that I felt in love with my husband Maurizio.

We met when I was 19 and he was 36. It was immediate attraction. I lied about my age, fearing to be too young to be taken seriously, so I said I was twenty. We never were engaged; instead, we lived together almost immediately. Not alone though: his parents had died, and the only elder family member left was his old uncle, a single man, retired army officer, who had lost an arm in World War II during an air bombing in the desert. So me, the Venetian country girl, became Venetian.

Me, him, Uncle, and Maurizio's son during school vacations, used to live in a large apartment at the last floor over Campiello della Cason, near the Church of San Cancian. At night all you could hear were the footsteps of people walking the narrow *calle* downstairs, and the clack of the two iron hooks on the bridge. People believed that beating those ancient metals would bring them luck even if those were used for hanging body parts of poor people condemned to death by the severe Serenissima justice.

Life then was sometimes hard and sometimes easy, but I was young. And Venice was all new, to be discovered—almost 40 years ago. Not so many tourists like today. So many small shops. I remember the smell of each place. One would only sell pork meat. Another one only milk and cheese. La Signora, a very kind lady, who used to run the tobacco shop, was a celebrity in the neighborhood, and people named the little square after her: "*Campiello della Natalina*." La Signora Maria, on the other hand, was the fruit and vegetable merchant in Rio Terà Barba Frutariol (a name that means "the uncle fruit seller on the street over the former canal"). She was a tall and sturdy woman who would always succeed in selling you more than you had on your list, confident in the fact that for centuries that was "the place" for that type of commerce. When she died, no one could believe it. We all thought she had to be immortal. Even today, her grandson has the same beautiful outdoors display of the most colorful and delicious of nature's gifts. You go and check.

Rialto Market was full of fish. Old Uncle Rico taught me how to cook it. The first time Maurizio brought home *schie*, the gray shrimps, I got so scared of having to touch, wash, and cook hundreds of jumping dark insect-looking aliens. Same when I first prepared *bovoleti*, the tiny snails, so abundant in spring along with the artichokes from Sant'Erasmo.

My husband made of me a Venetian. This mainland girl was patiently trained in all traditional habits, so that I could be recognized as one. But I also needed to be Venetian my way, an *Impiraressa*, a bead stringer, as beads were my acquired passion in the following years. That was the ultimate dream he helped me fulfill.

Maurizio died on the 21st of September 2017. He left me the Venetian heritage as a gift. He used to drink his spritz with bitters, but there was nothing bitter about our life together.

Biography

Marisa Convento, the "Impiraressa," is a Venetian glass jewelry designer, recently awarded by the city of Venice as one of the best local artisans always first in line defending the traditions. Since 2007 Marisa manages the bottega *Venetian Dreams, a small workshop that has become a meeting point for residents and visitors from all over the world, reviewed by many magazines, guides, and blogs.*

"Tabarroshop" by Monica Daniele

The *tabarro* is a piece of clothing that clothes a person in the fullest sense of the word. The five or six meters of warm, light fabric, resistant to rain and wind, offer an easy shelter so it is a pleasure wrapping and shielding ourselves from the weather. Many wonder what *tabarro* means. The garment, which comes from the past, can even today fit properly into our wardrobe, as it performs its functions of practicality, elegance, refinement, as it emulates sensibilities of nature and the environment.

Giacomo Puccini immortalized the term in a shadowy and twilit opera, *Il Tabarro*, which premiered with great success on December 14, 1918, at the Metropolitan Theater in New York.

In the opera, Giorgetta, wife of Michele who owns a boat in the Seine, falls in love with Luigi, a young longshoreman who every evening, attracted by the faint glow of a lit match, reaches for her, protected by obscurity. Michele, who sees his love illusions gradually collapsing, tries to awaken in his wife's soul the passion of the past, reminding her of the child whose brief existence had accompanied their love: those were the happy days when Giorgetta and her son were looking for shelter in his cloak, the wide cloak that the boatman used to wear. The rest I leave as a surprise for readers.

So, in 1994 in the magical city of Venice, as a Venetian designer I followed my instincts to invent new work for myself. Not so enthusiastic about having to do a tourist job, as often happens after school studies, and passionate about fashion and costumes, I fantasized about giving new life to these nefarious, mysterious-looking cloaks, perfect to wear from autumn to late winter in a city perennially flooded by humid air, where you walk on foot and follow pathways that have remained intact over time.

Albert Gardin, Venetian publisher with a catalog of over 1,200 titles on the history and literature of Venice, ancient and contemporary, in 1997 brought to light and published a very important work by Giacomo Casanova, his *Iliad* by Homer translated into Venetian. Working alongside me in my *tabarro* shop on Calle Scaleter, he discovered that this illustrious character had walked down this street in 1776.

A natural accompaniment to the age-old *tabarri* are the hats, which are also making a well-deserved comeback, serving both to warm us and protect us. Dressing up in a cloak is a bit like restoring the city's immortality, even if it falls well within the canons of modern and functional style. They also provide a sense of freedom outside the box, undermining the globalist clothing market, calling its values into question. And that is why those who dress "*in tabarro*" are also expressing a philosophical idea of what it means to make fashion.

Biography

Monica Daniele studied painting at the Accademia di Belle Arte di Venezia and now runs her shop Tabarro San Marco. In a shop reminiscent of yesteryear, you can find and try her collection of tabarri, *hats, and accessories.*

Tabarrosanmarco.com

Monicadaniele.com

Facebook: tabarromonicadaniele

"My One Consolation... " by Gregory Dowling

So, yes, it was love at first sight. This short piece is about that first sight and how, as always with true love, it changed my life. It will contain a few clichés about the city because if you decide, when writing about Venice, that you are going to avoid all clichés you are not likely to get very far. You will probably find yourself still stuck in the station at Mestre, gazing at a view of railway sidings and high-rise flats.

So I will begin with two clichés, which perhaps gain in curiosity value by being set down side by side, since they apparently contradict one another. The first is the declaration of most visitors—since Byron's time at least—that we know the city before we ever go there. Indeed, the French writer Michel Tournier says that one travels to Venice in order to *recognize* it, rather than to see it. We know it from paintings and poems and films and Instagram photos and YouTube videos and ice cream ads. (Goethe, never one to be outdone when it came to knowing things, declared that his first sight of Venice carried him right back to his infancy and the gift of a toy gondola from his father.)

The second cliché is that one's first glimpse of Venice is unforgettably astonishing.

The real curiosity-value in these two clichés lies in the fact that they are both true. The tourist's amazement at the view from the station steps is far more convincingly sincere than, say, a display of dropped-jaw and wide-eyes at a first glimpse of the *Mona Lisa*.

And this is why so many books about the town by foreigners begin with this moment of arrival and its strange combination of déjà-vu and revelation. I can well remember my own surprise in July 1979 (and here I go, winding in to the conventional opening, like the river Marzenego lazily snaking its way into the lagoon) when I realized the train was apparently shooting out across the sea. One moment there was a view of scrubby wasteland to the left and the hulking tubes, drums, and chimneys of an oil refinery to the right, and the next—water.

Well, of course I had expected water. But not that much. Not all together and so suddenly.

I was only changing trains at Venice, being on my way from Naples, where I had been teaching for four months, to stay with an old school friend in Treviso before returning to England for the summer. Of course I should have changed at Mestre, but of the names Mestre-Venezia on my ticket, it was only the second that had stuck in my mind; the other meant nothing to me. (And this condition of insignificant obscurity is something the Mestrini have learnt to put up with: there is no more melancholy expression than that on the face of tourists who discover that their cut-price luxury hotel is not on a picturesque side canal in Venice's outer quarters but on a main road of the Serenissima's ugly sister.) And, my ignorance of matters geographical and historical being sublime in its range and depth, I had not expected much from this simple change of trains. Perhaps the distant glimpse of an odd *campanile* or dome, as at Florence station.

Now I found myself gazing out to the left at the lagoon, a vast expanse of olive oil green, unbroken but for occasional clumps of poles and a few islands, like hazy pencil strokes on the horizon. I looked across the compartment to the right; the sinking sun transformed the water to a gleaming expanse of unruffled silver: a sheet of taut tinfoil, so calmly aglow that it seemed to be exuding light that the sky borrowed. "A whole bunch of water," as an American girl in the compartment remarked.

When I got off the train, I discovered there was a connection to Treviso in fifteen minutes. Just time to go and see if there was an interesting view outside the station.

There was.

I stood there, my army surplus rucksack bowing me into a figure seven, my two tattered hold-alls by my side, and I gazed at a view made famous by Canaletto: a church with a pillared porch and green dome across the canal; buildings contemplating their own reflections; a steady bustle of small crafts; a babble of voices in all languages. And gondolas: black, slim, and prancing.

"Wow, it's just like the movies," said a voice to my left. I can't be sure now whether it was a young or old voice, male or female. I just remember that those were the first words I heard while staring at this scene.

Or maybe I said them to myself. Because this is the first impression Venice makes on all of us: she is just what we have been

35

led to expect. And of course this surprises us. It is like getting a glimpse of a film star and discovering that she is as beautiful in the flesh as she appears on the screen. In general we live in a constant expectation of disappointment: the beach will never be as spotless as the brochure shows, the hotel is bound to be clad in scaffolding, the food will be oily or meager.... Venice paradoxically defeats our expectations by living so superbly up to them. And this explains the contradiction in those two clichés.

But my initial surprise—and I think everyone's—had another source as well. The city was *intrinsically* astonishing: however many paintings or films I might have seen, nothing had prepared me for the sheer improbability of Venice's situation. All that water. This, I notice, is something that many visitors, right back to Thomas Coryat in the seventeenth century, stress: "Such is the rareness of the situation of Venice that it doth even amaze and drive into admiration all strangers that upon their first arrival behold the same."

As the guidebooks always state, anyone who does not arrive from the sea is approaching Venice by the back door. The bridge across the lagoon is a two-mile suppository thrust into Venice's posterior. However, nowadays this is the entrance for nearly all visitors, and it must be said that Venice's scullery and back stairs are more magnificent than the state ballrooms of most cities. The fact is that there is no dull approach to Venice.

Those who come by car make their way round the tangle of flyovers and roundabouts outside Mestre suddenly to find themselves shooting out through two ceremonious pillars into the lagoon, aiming straight for the green dome of San Simeone Piccolo and the sturdy geometrical lines of the Campanile of St. Mark's apparently right behind it. Those who fly catch a wonderful glimpse (particularly if they are sitting on the right hand side of the plane) of the city, laid out below them in the lagoon, its curving cluster of rust-red roofs and grey domes sharply framed by the silvery-green of the water, the slender ribbon of the Lido providing a final line of limitation to the east. From the airport a waterbus will take them down the canal that lies parallel to the runway, where in hot weather locals sunbathe on small oily beaches; the boat then heads out across the lagoon, briefly slowing down as it passes a small privately-owned island and then again as it chugs down the Grand Canal of

Murano. And then, after swinging round the back entrance to the Arsenale, past the island of San Pietro and Sant'Elena, there comes the final grand approach: if you time it right, the city will actually lay out a flickering red carpet of reflected sunset for you all the way across the Bacino di San Marco to the entrance of the Grand Canal.

Venice *is* improbable. It is built where no one in their right minds would ever dream of building a city. And this sense of improbability does not wear off as we get to know the city better. We continue to be struck—amazed or amused—by its persistent oddity: front doors with seaweedy steps, shoppers crossing the main road to the market standing upright in a crowded gondola, invalids being carted in wheelbarrow-like stretchers to the nearest canal, traffic lights hanging above an intersection of waterways, washing lines strung from Renaissance balconies over scummy depths. Such things for anyone not born to them will never lose their surreal charm.

Of course we all react differently to this immediate impression of implausibility. I remember that as I stood there, sweating under my ill-packed rucksack, I felt a highly inappropriate sense of lightness. It is probably an exaggeration to say that I knew I had arrived home at last (though there are travel writers who have talked about Venice's moist closeness as beckoning to the fetus-instinct in us all); I did know that here was a place I was going to feel at ease in.

For a start it was a total contrast to Naples. I had enjoyed my four-month stint down there, but had been glad to leave at the end of it, before my hearing suffered irreparable damage. Naples greets you, as you emerge from its main station, by clobbering you with a vicious cosh of decibels: an unmusical medley of voices, shouting, crying, calling, a rumbling of buses, a raging of cars, a roaring of motorbikes, and everywhere, as a kind of manic background chorus, a whingeing and whining of car horns. Your first impression is that you must have walked into the immediate aftermath of some cataclysm; gradually you come to realize that Neapolitan life is always conducted at top volume. It is probably why they are the best gesturers in the world: often it is their only hope of making themselves understood.

The scene I was contemplating was not silent. Far from it. But the noise was relaxed—and, most importantly, it was mainly human.

A harmonious mélange of unraised voices. The throbbing of the boats was definitely a *sottofondo*. There were a few obvious touts around—guides, porters, and hotel reps—but whereas in Naples you are never too scruffy to be denied their attention, here they gave me no more than the most cursory of glances. My tattered jeans (I had made a minor name for myself in Naples by being the only person in the town still wearing flares) told them all they needed to know. I suppose the Neapolitans are more open-minded in this respect; but I welcomed the chance of pester-free anonymity.

After another couple of minutes of silent gazing I made my way back into the station. My first visit to Venice was over.

A similar five-minute gawp from the entrance to Victoria Station probably would not give you the feeling you now knew London. But this sense of immediate revelation is one of Venice's great charms. It turns us into instant connoisseurs. We all feel we have been granted the chance of a special and even intimate relationship. She may not have revealed her all yet, but she is definitely giving us the come-on.

And so the following few days I commuted in from Treviso and did what so many first time visitors do: I drifted around the place. Of course, most visitors prior to this century did so quite literally, lounging in their gondolas and watching the *palazzi* float past. Nowadays, a gondola trip is a carefully bargained high point to the visit, with one eye on the view and the other divided between one's watch and the holiday budget figures.

For the rest of the time most of us do our drifting on foot; we may be press-ganged into guided tours of the main sights, marched around the museums, led in bewilderment past the great canvases of the Doge's Palace and be force-fed the dates of the mosaics of St. Mark's, but the principal and most memorable of our early experiences is the mapless wandering around the back streets and minor *campielli* of the city. It is here, as we photograph mangy cats beside well heads or sip our wine in greasy back street taverns, that we can cherish our illusion that we have escaped the trite tourist tracks, that we have got to know the "real" Venice: she is revealing to us—and to us alone—her tattered but frilly underwear.

This instinctive urge to seek out a "real" Venice is, to some extent, peculiar to our age. It is of course mainly due to a desire to distinguish ourselves from the herd, from the unthinking mass of tourists content with the TripAdvisor view of the city. (And nowhere do we feel more threatened with forcible inclusion into the herd than in St. Mark's Square.) But it is perhaps also due to a panic-stricken desire, amidst the overwhelming strangeness of the city, to anchor ourselves to some vestige of actuality; Venice may be cinematically spectacular at first sight, we say to ourselves, but we have now discovered the simpler, earthier charms of her back streets—those sights that the Italians describe as "*caratteristici*."

It didn't take me long to realize what an illusion this was. When I returned to Treviso in the evening and told my old school friend casually of the quiet, little square I'd discovered, quite remote from the tourist paths, he of course already knew it. When I mentioned the Church of Sant'Angelo Raffaele, he asked me if I'd enjoyed the Guardi paintings on the organ and if I'd been round the corner to see the Church of San Nicolò dei Mendicoli. I had no idea who Guardi was and, of course, had not seen the other church he mentioned.

I began to understand that it would take more than a few day trips to be able to pass myself off as an expert on all things Venetian. So it was perhaps then that the idea began to grow in me that I would have to live in Venice for a while and steep myself in its art, history, and literature, as well as its food, drink, and gossip, not to mention its sights, sounds, and smells; and then I might be able to impress (or, more probably, bore) people with my casual knowingness. At the time I was probably thinking of spending a few months in the city, maybe a whole year, if lucky. To that purpose, some months later, I got myself a job in a language school in Verona, within easy reach of Venice. And just a year and half later I moved to Venice itself.

That was 37 years ago. I'm now beginning to feel that I do know something about the city. I certainly know who Guardi is, what is in the Church of San Nicolò dei Mendicoli, and which streets to take to avoid *acqua alta* and tourist flows. And I feel confident enough to write novels set in Venice, with Venetian protagonists. Of course, I'll never achieve true Venetianness. For example, I'll probably always be offered the tourist menu in restaurants, and I'll never be able to speak Venetian like a native—like my own children, that is to say.

When it comes down to it, the one advantage I have over native Venetians (like these same children of mine) is that they have never had a first sight of Venice. It's certainly not a meager consolation.

Biography

Gregory Dowling grew up in Bristol, England, and graduated from Oxford University. From 1979 to 1981 he taught in language schools in Naples, Siena, and Verona. In 1981 he moved to Venice, where he has lived ever since. Since 1985 he has worked at Ca' Foscari University of Venice, where he is now Associate Professor of American Literature. In addition to his novels (six thrillers), he has done numerous translations from Italian into English, has co-edited two anthologies of poetry, written a book on American narrative poetry, a book on the English verb system, and a guidebook to Byron's Venice, as well as numerous scholarly articles on British and American literature. He is editor of the British section of the Italian poetry-journal Semicerchio. *For many years he wrote and regularly updated the sightseeing pages of the* Time Out Guide to Venice. *His most recent novels, set in eighteenth century Venice, are* Ascension *and* The Four Horsemen.

More information can be found on his website: gregorydowling.com.

"*Paradiso Perduto*" by Shannon Essa

Lovers of Venice, imagine this: I am visiting Venice for the first time, at the end of my very first trip to Italy, in the Fall of 1998. I am traveling with a friend and we have partied, been hung over, recovered with red wine and pasta, and partied again through Rome, Florence, Sorrento, and a bit of Tuscany. I am already totally enthralled by everything I have experienced so far. I kind of know a little about Venice when I arrive. Kind of.

But as we all know, nothing can really prepare you for the sensory overload that Venice thrusts upon the visitor. On my first visit, it rained constantly, there was *acqua alta*, and it was oppressively humid. My friend and I were not getting along after three weeks of traveling together and now smashed into a tiny double room in Campo Santo Stefano. Still, even though the sun was not shining, and even though the vibe was not harmonious, I totally and completely fell in love with Venice.

My mind was being blown in many ways. My friend and I bought rubber boots and splashed through Piazza San Marco in knee high water and drank Champagne—not Prosecco!—in expensive hotel bars that I would rarely go to now. It was like being in a dream. One afternoon, taking a break from my friend, I stopped in a bar close to our hotel to write in my journal. My seat was at the window; the window had a view out onto the narrow *calle*, an antiques shop, and a butcher. While I sat there, the bored young antiques salesman came into the bar and ordered a whiskey with one ice cube in it, drank it quickly, and returned to the shop that no one came into while I was there. A few minutes later, a senior woman with a little dog went into the butcher shop; customer and butcher emerged, came into the bar and had an *ombra*—those little glasses of wine that used to be sold all over Venice—together. The woman went on her way, and the butcher went back to work. The intimacy of it all, after years of living in a big city, was like some kind of tonic to me. I was hooked. I went back again for a week six months later, then for a month. Eventually I went to live there for a year. Drinking an *ombra*, watching other people drink them while socializing for ten minutes or for an hour, became part of the fabric of my life.

I was lucky to experience the tail end of what was a network of little, insular communities, each with its own markets, bakers, bars, and hardware stores. The sense of community was so important to me. Even if I was not really a true part of it, I watched it, enthralled, from various perches in bars and cafes, at the Rialto Market, in the public squares where parents and grandparents would hang out to chat while watching the kids play.

Some of this community is still there. Many of the shops and bakers and hardware stores are not. For years I thought that these little shops would never go away, and that the little communities would somehow survive. I was, sadly, totally wrong. Business owners retire, or get priced out, or their clientele disappears; but the shops replacing the service-oriented stores that close are not for the people living in Venice. They are for the pass-through people. People like me. I have always been a pass-through. But until very recently, I did not worry too much about it. I thought I was giving back something. Now I am not so sure.

I have a good friend, Colleen, who was attached to Venice as much as I was. It was how we first met, loving Venice, and our friendship grew over several trips where we wandered purposely and aimlessly at the same time. We always poopooed the people who said Venice was Disneyland, or that it was too crowded, because we knew how to get away from those crowds. We defended the "real" Venice and insisted, correctly at the time, that it was possible to find it. In 2004, she wrote me a note that I recently found in a book about Venice. The writer Donna Leon had told some reporter somewhere that Venice was on a path to mass tourism that could not be reversed. "That is pessimistic," Colleen wrote. Neither of us believed it. But Donna Leon was right. At least she is right, right now.

As I am writing this, the May 1 holiday is approaching, and the government of Venice is going to apparently segregate the tourists and the local people. They are using turnstiles to count the arrivals. Venice HAS become Disneyland. Crowds are nothing new to me; there have always been a ton of people clogging the main thoroughfares and massive groups following an umbrella around Piazza San Marco. This tsunami of crowds is getting bigger every year and forming into an endless series of destructive crests. Everyone knows it is too much for the city and what is going on is not sustainable, yet the ships keep arriving, the Biennale art festival keeps growing, the *alimentari* shops keep closing and turning into fast food joints and "Made in China" glass and mask shops. Most of the people working in Venice now live on the mainland, and many of them do not even care. They have better shops for food in Mestre these days. There are backyards and peace and quiet. There are no tourists in Mestre.

Every time I visit Venice now, I find one of my favorite places gone—either turned into a different kind of restaurant (the beloved Fiaschetteria Toscana restaurant closed last year and was replaced by a Burger King) or with Chinese owners at the helm. It is a game of dominoes, and soon there will be no old standbys left.

What do we do? What can we do? I wish I could do more to save this place that I fell in love with twenty years ago. Venice has been around for millennia. Maybe the city will return to the way it used to be in 1950, or a thousand years ago. Venice will outlive all of us, that is for sure. We can only hope that there is more to the future than what we are seeing now.

Biography

A California native, Shannon Essa spent over three decades working in the wine and food industries in various incarnations— cooking, serving, educating, and marketing. She has also spent a lot of time in Venice and co-wrote a guidebook to eating there, Chow! Venice, *with Ruth Edenbaum. Shannon now organizes small group wine and food tours in Italy, Spain, Croatia, Slovenia, and Portugal for her company GrapeHops Tours. She is currently on a quest to relocate to Spain.*

Grapehops.com facebook.com/GrapeHops

"Tiramisu with Attila" by Roger Feuerman

I sat at my usual table at the renowned Caffè Florian, a neo-baroque Venetian institution in Piazza San Marco, frequented by tourists and locals alike. Stirring my espresso with a small silver spoon, I glanced in the mirror hoping I looked half as handsome as Casanova, the rogue who had most likely sat in this chair. Alas, that was not to be the case.

As I delighted in listening to the orchestra playing just outside, I scribbled some notes on my pad, all the while keeping one eye on the door. My guest was expected any minute now.

Would he live up to my expectations?

A short time later the bronze figures atop the Piazza's clock tower struck the bell signaling noon. Staring down into the black abyss of my espresso, I wondered if he would appear at all.

I looked up and there he stood, framed by the caffè's doorway.

He was a short man, well, at least shorter than I imagined. But his broad chest somehow made up for that. He had small, piercing eyes, a trim beard, and wore a fur-lined vest and hat, an outfit appropriate for winter's Carnevale. But this was June.

I stood up and nodded, so he would know who I was. He saw me but didn't nod back. From his demeanor I wished there had been a "check your dagger at the door" sign. He strode over to my table and stood there, taking my measure.

"I didn't mean to be presumptuous," I said, "but I ordered you some tiramisu and espresso, as I expect you're weary from your trip."

Satisfied, somewhat, he sat down. I sat, too.

"Thank you for accepting my invitation, Mister Hun, especially since this is on such short notice, though I have been thinking of you for months. I'm sure you're eager for me to fill in on the *who, whys,* and *whats,* so let me begin."

"First, the *who.* My full name is Roger Feuerman. You may call me Roger. I am a writer by trade. I'm working on a historical fiction novel about Venice, in fact. It's such a magical city, don't you know. But, as we both know, you really don't know, since you have never been here before."

The barbarian kept his eyes on me, not the confection before him.

"So that is who I am, Mister Hun. May I call you Attila?" He responded with a grunt. I took that as a 'no.'"

"As to *why* I asked you to journey all the way here from the fifth century, well, it's because I wanted you to get to know the wonder of Venice, a city that floats on water. I must confess that I'm addicted to it, returning again and again for inspiration. Mister Hun, you haven't tasted your tiramisu. It's an impossibly creamy layered confection."

My guest's look said "Get to the point."

"So, let me finally get to the *what*, and tell you what you'll be experiencing here. First, where will you reside? I could have put you up in a charming *locanda*, a quiet place on a side canal. Instead I chose the opposite, getting you a suite in the most famous of Venetian hotels, the Gritti Palace. Standing on its balcony overlooking the Grand Canal you'll feel like an emperor. Appropriate, I thought, as you are one, a tribal emperor, once lording over lands that encompassed much of Central and Eastern Europe.

"Then, starting the next morning, you shall experience Venice's sights, its sounds, its smells, its tastes, its very feel.

"Monday, we'll get a peek at this city's daily life. We'll watch women hanging their wash over the alleyways; gondoliers singing the same songs their great-great-grandfathers sang; nuns conversing about the wisdom of the pastor's sermon; children kicking balls against ancient brick walls; bakers opening their doors, enticing passersby with the smell of fresh bread. Perhaps we'll even try a pastry there.

"Tuesday, we'll get a bit of culture, going to the Accademia Museum and viewing the masterpieces painted by Renaissance giants Canaletto, Bellini, and Titian. Then, that night I've reserved seats for us at La Fenice, a jewel box of an opera house. We'll dress up… or, or you could just wear what you're wearing.

"Wednesday, we'll immerse ourselves in Venice's political past, going to the Doge's Palace, the seat of its power. We'll gaze in wonder at the Great Council room where they made the laws. And we'll see what happened to those who ran afoul of them, by crossing the Bridge of Sighs and standing in the prison's cold, dank cells.

"Thursday, we'll explore the Rialto Market, teeming with its fresh vegetables, meats, and fish. And we'll have some fun haggling with the merchants of Venice for leather goods, coming away with 'our prize' for only half price, but never wise to the fact it had been marked up triple.

"Friday, we'll go to the *squero* of San Trovaso and observe a gondola being built out of eight different kinds of wood. Afterwards, we'll hire one and ride down the *Canale Grande,* passing by the magnificent palazzos of Venice's noble class, not built of wood, but of the finest marble.

"Saturday, we'll walk the cobblestone maze of *calli* and discover some of Casanova's old haunts, where we'll drink Prosecco and sing songs shoulder to shoulder with the locals. Then, as evening falls, we'll do a little gambling in this city that was the site of the world's first state-run casino, Il Ridotto.

"Sunday we'll repent and go to church at the famed Basilica across the *piazza*. We'll marvel at the oriental-inspired domed exterior as well as the interior encrusted with golden mosaics that gleam by the light of prayer candles. Or maybe we'll pick another famous church at which to confess our sins, the Pietà, called Vivaldi's church, since many of his compositions were written and performed there.

"Quite a week, quite a week you'll experience. But no need to thank me for this, Mister Hun. For it is I who should be thanking you. We all should. Because *you* are why we're here, in this impossibly beautiful place."

Attila's eyes widened.

"That's right. You see, when you invaded northern Italy, terrorizing village after village, you spread fear everywhere. Enough fear that the people in the mainland towns of Aquileia, Treviso, and Padua sought refuge in the only place you wouldn't pursue them, the marshes of the lagoon, where history records that they were left alone in their small fishing villages, alone to grow."

Attila's eyes narrowed.

"Ironic, don't you think, that your scorched-earth campaign led to the one-day rise of a world economic powerhouse, controlling trade routes that brought spices and silks from China to Paris, Amsterdam, and London.

"That your army's devastation led to the building of a Venetian Navy of 16,000 ships, who flexed her military might as 'Queen of the Adriatic Sea.'

"That your wrecking ball of a crusade led to delightful masked balls of Carnevale.

"That the clang of your swords led to the clang of bells in one hundred and forty-one churches in Venice and its lagoon islands.

"That the tramping of your hordes' feet led to the dancing of the minuet in grand *palazzi*.

"That the flight of your archers' arrows led to the bowing of violins in the piazzas.

"That the fires that you once set led to celebratory fireworks over Venice as she 'marries the sea' each June.

"Yes, Mister Hun, from fear sprang an empire that rivaled yours and surpassed it, a 'Most Serene Republic' that prospered for a thousand years, with its capital the second largest city of its day."

Attila grunted.

"So look around you, Mister Hun, see the 30 million tourists a year that enjoy the splendors of Venice."

Attila sneered.

"Sneer if you will. But please take no offense. I do not mean to insult you, just to present this observation: that you, yes you, are 'the beast that birthed the beauty' that is Venice."

Attila eased his hand onto his dagger. I eased my hand onto my espresso cup, took a sip, gently set it down, and continued.

"Mister Hun, they say that 'curiosity killed the cat, satisfaction brought him back.' So, if you don't mind me asking, after knowing what you now know, would you do what you did again?"

The muscles on Attila's neck stood out.

"Would you wreak havoc and inflict pain on so many people?"

He rose from his chair.

"You haven't touched your dessert, Mister Hun."

He glared at me, slowly pulled out his dagger… and plunged it into the table in front of me. Then he turned abruptly and marched out.

As I watched him go I hoped, at least, he was soothed by the orchestra's music as he crossed the square… and evaporated. Gone. And so was the dagger. Now both living only in this writer's imagination.

49

But Attila had "passed the audition." He was irascible enough to become a villain in my novel.

I pulled his tiramisu closer to me and lifted a silver forkful of this Venetian creation to my waiting mouth.

It was impossibly delicious.

Biography

Roger Feuerman doesn't actually live in Venice. But after ten plus journeys there, Venice certainly lives in him. He is currently completing a historical fiction novel that takes place in its palazzi, *canals, and blind alleyways, chronicling the amorous adventures and misadventures of its masked inhabitants, all of whom would be intrigued with a rogue's latest tryst; few of whom would be interested that Roger, the writer of their story, was previously an advertising copywriter, winning a Lion at the Venice International Film Festival, and who also once penned a "get out the vote" spot for a former President. He is a member of the Dramatist Guild of America.*

"Lonely in a Crowd" by Bob Fusillo

Venetian shopkeepers and waiters are often lonely. They almost never see the same people twice. Vast numbers of tourists peek into a shop, and leave. Some buy something, and leave. They eat, and leave. Back to the cruise ship or the bus. All never to return. Waiters in busy restaurants don't have time or inclination to really look at patrons. I remember a time when we returned to a restaurant a second night and had the same waiter. We mentioned last night's dinner and he looked surprised and said, "You've been here before?"

So it is not surprising that after a second or third visit, everything changes. Suddenly you are friends. At smaller restaurants you become almost family. You are served aperitifs when you arrive. The waiters bombard you with questions about America and their hopes to go there. They confide in you about their lives—who they are dating, their travels, upcoming weddings. The chef comes out to say hello. Often, like *Mamma*, they will tell you what you must eat and drink. And they remember your tastes in wine, in food, in tables. The coffee shops remember, from year to year, your desires in coffee brands and even the grind. The butcher knows which thickness you want for your bacon. The pizza place knows, as you come down the *calle*, which pizza and wine you will want (after the on-the-house spritz).

Some instances of flattering memory stand out. It was our regular habit on Sunday mornings to stand on the bridge near our flat and share a Prosecco while looking down the canal and its environs. One day as we came down the bridge, the owner of the restaurant at its foot came out and said, "You make me happy. You are enjoying life." Then every week she would meet us and chat. It became a pleasant ritual. She hid how ill she was.

Then one spring she died. It left a hole in our Sundays. One day we made a reservation at the restaurant, and the young lady who took our names, said, "You must be Bob and Edith. Roberta used to talk about you often. She admired your happiness and fondness for each other." To be remembered by Roberta was lovely: for the young woman to remember us by way of Roberta's stories was amazing. We have not seen that bridge the same way since.

Biography

Bob Fusillo is a regular visitor to Venice since the late fifties, and for the past fifteen years, two to three months living there fall and spring.

"Sounds of Venice" by Edith Fusillo

Very few question the visual beauty of Venice—at every turn there is something interesting, and often breathtaking, to see. My husband and I have been coming to Venice for a couple of months at a time for several years. We always rent the same apartment, and while most of our visits are in the Fall, we have also stayed in the city in the spring. Even though we have been coming for years, no trip fails to yield some new discovery to feast the eyes upon.

As residents, though, it is not the sights of Venice that we feel most familiar with: it is the sounds. Because it is extremely old and very crowded, most of the "streets" are only about ten feet wide, and some are so narrow that it is impossible to walk through them with an opened umbrella. Our own apartment is on the oldest residential street in Venice, and the buildings on either side were constructed in the 1400s. The huge black beams of the original street still loom. The apartment goes the whole way through our building, making a narrow place with windows in the front and in the back. The front street is about ten feet wide, but the back street, which is really no more than an alley with no access from any building on the street except the restaurant over which we live, is only six feet across at the most. Thus, the proximity of the apartments make for an audial environment that is as much a part of our Venice as canals and gondolas. Because there are no cars in Venice, at certain times of the night the silence is stunning, making the sounds of the city all the more noticeable.

At all hours, the sound most constant is the click, click of suitcase wheels on the cobblestones. Unlike many cities where hotels are clustered in one central area, there are tiny hotels scattered throughout Venice, so someone is always either going or coming with his luggage. Shopping carts, called *carrelli*, also have wheels, but their sound is distinctly different from those of luggage wheels.

For us, the day in the neighborhood, beautiful or not, begins and ends with the sound of the shutters. It is an absolute custom in Venice to close the shutters at night, and open them again in the morning. Our neighbor just across the way from our bedroom is an early riser, and the sound of her squeaking shutter hinge at 6:15 is the signal that day is about to begin—no need even to consult the clock. Shortly thereafter, the shutters in the next apartment swing open, and we hear the sounds of the breakfast dishes being set out. In the front, the lady of the house is somewhat later in opening her shutters, and when she does so, she always adjusts the Venetian blinds (yes, Virginia, there really ARE Venetian blinds) so that they are open exactly one third of their height.

Shutters are a boon when a storm is raging through the city, keeping the rain from dripping in through the not-very-efficient windows. Venetian residents close the shutters both to keep out the summer's heat and winter's cold, but also to afford a measure of privacy in a city where little privacy is possible. A walk down any street allows one to hear every toilet flushing, every television show, every aspiring opera singer's vocalizing. For us, used to the more generous spaces between dwellings in our suburban neighborhood back home, closing the shutters makes us feel cooped up, especially in our dark first floor apartment, where the sun only filters through as far as the window boxes, and that only late in the day. (We often greet the woman across the way in the front as we both lean out the window to water our plants.) So we have worked out a compromise by closing certain shutters just enough so that the neighbors cannot look directly in on us lounging in bed far after respectable people would be up and doing something useful.

Because ours is a major route to the school in Santa Maria Formosa, the sound of school children making their way to and from school is an every-morning affair during the week. They squawk and shout, push and shove, but most of all they laugh. Many of them are accompanied by their parents, and the friendly shouts of "*ciao*" reach us all over the apartment. Venetians cannot say "*ciao*" just once: it is always in multiples of at least three and sometimes as many as five.

Another absolutely recognizable sound is the high-pitched squeak of the clothesline being pulled across the space as clothes are hung out to dry. Every home in Venice, I believe, has a washing machine. It is a rare rental apartment that does not include one. By contrast, I don't know anyone in Venice, or for that matter anywhere in Italy (except our American friends Carl and Sally) who own a dryer. Until this year, we did not even see them for sale in the appliance section of major stores. Italians seem morally opposed to the very idea of a dryer, though most places have no room for one even if the owner was inclined to install one. Even fairly good-sized hotels have their lines stretched out across several windows high above the ground, and it is not unusual to see the hotel linens, including sheets, swinging in the sunshine. I have come to listen for the weather report not on the TV, but by the squeak of the clothesline, indicating that the housewife above or beside me is confident that there will be no rain today.

Closely related to the clothesline's song is the noise, often more felt than actually heard, of a washing machine in one apartment or another, always during the spin cycle. One family in an adjoining apartment has a small child, and the washing machine goes pretty much constantly, as one would expect in a household with a baby. However, even our machine runs quite a lot, though there are only two adults in our apartment. The load size is quite small compared to the giant Maytag I have in the States. And, because the washing machines here heat the water for each cycle, doing a load of laundry can take almost two hours. Careful planning is necessary to make sure the laundry is washed in time to take advantage of a sunny day. In late fall, with notably cooler, damper weather, the routine is hang the laundry out, leave it for three days, bring it in, set up the folding drying rack, hang the laundry on it for three days, and then start over. I confess that in Venice we typically wear our clothes for much longer between washings than in Atlanta.

The sounds of renovation are a constant in Venice. The city is always under "*restauro*" somewhere, and here in our neighborhood, both the apartment immediately above us and the one immediately beside us are under renovation. Hammering, drilling, the screech of saws through marble—this is a given. Add to that the ever-present reconstruction of the streets, with the digging up of huge cobblestones, and the noise of "progress" is everywhere.

In our apartment, there are some sounds that are very particularly ours. Because we live over a restaurant that frequently has large groups of young tourists, we recognize immediately the sudden gathering of voices just below our front window. This signals that a group will be having lunch or dinner below us, and is a warning that this is NOT a good time to go downstairs for a meal. At some point during the lunch or dinner, we will hear the itinerant musicians, typically an accordion and a clarinet, playing music for the enjoyment of the group. We can know the nationality of the group by the choice of music played. And always, when the diners are very young and very enthusiastic, we hear the sound of at least one unfortunate soul rushing out the door and down to the bridge over the canal to get rid of the excess wine that (usually) she has consumed. Then, a burst of noise as the group leaves for other locales, followed by the clink of bottles being bagged up for the garbage man.

The garbage system in Venice is remarkable. Most of us in the States are used to having our garbage collected once or twice a week at most. In Venice, each night or early morning, every household places its garbage outside the door in a plastic bag. It is then collected every day except Sunday. This is a cumbersome process, as everything in Venice involves moving large carts over bridge after bridge. The garbage collector pushes his cart through every tiny street, throwing the bags of refuse into his cart. When it is full, the cart goes to the nearest square with a canal—in our case to Campo de la Guerra, where it is emptied onto a waiting garbage boat to be taken to the mainland for disposal. Because Venice requires that refuse be separated into garbage, glass/plastic/metal, and paper, the sounds of colletion are immediately recognizable. In particular, throwing bags of glass into the cart can be jarring early in the morning. We often hear tourists, particularly American and British tourists, whine about how dirty Venice is. We, on the other hand, are constantly amazed at how clean the streets are, given the density of the housing and the number of rather inconsiderate visitors the city hosts each day.

Another sound that our apartment "enjoys" is the regular Sunday morning visits to the apartment next door of *Mamma*. Sometime just after early Mass and before the family goes out to dinner somewhere, there is about an hour of non-stop harangue. I don't know whether it is the wife's or the husband's mother, but she shouts angrily, non-stop, for at least an hour, interrupted practically not at all by the occasional modulated responses of husband or wife, none of which seems to register with *Mamma*. Sometimes the raging is about local politics, sometimes about the way the children behave, sometimes on other topics. *Mamma* orates loudly, punctuating her discourse with a smack, which I once thought might be a slap of a person, but which I now believe to be a newspaper or a palm against a table. There is no pause, no breath, only on and on.

And of course, when husband and wife choose to disagree with one another in *Mamma's* absence, we are privy to every clipped word. This closeness has on occasion proved to be charming in its way: the woman across the alley has been babysitting for her grandchild since the baby was born. Every morning I have listened to her talk gently to the baby, sometimes singing, and after three years the child now is able to respond. It is sweet, and I eavesdrop shamelessly on the lovely woman as she socializes and educates the child. And I have picked up a good bit of idiomatic Italian from this grandma.

And of course, there are the bells. Venice is a city of churches—there is a church in practically every square of any size, and almost every church has bells. We live between two squares, each with its own bell tower, and about equidistant between the bells of the Campanile in San Marco and those of the Church of SS. Giovanni e Paolo. Every day at certain times, and all day Sunday, there are the bells. We love them, even when they disturb our sleep.

And so, when others are looking at their photos of each other sitting on the *vaporetto*, or thumbing through their picture postcard views of Venice from a gondola, we tend to remember the sounds of Calle del Paradiso. These are the sounds that make it, for us, home.

Biography

Edith D. Fusillo, Ph,D.

In 2001 I retired from twenty-five years of teaching English as a Second Language to adults at Georgia Institute of Technology. In all that time, I had only three students from Italy; but for many years my husband and I had been visiting Venice for the one week a year that I had off. When I retired, we decided the appropriate way to celebrate my retirement and my 60th birthday was to go to, of course, Venice. As my husband researched hotels, he quickly determined that for the price of a hotel for a week, we could take an apartment for a month. And so we did. He was attracted to one apartment's website in particular because of the quirky background music. And so we came to rent from, and to call friend, Piero Bellini. Over the years he has been our guide, translator, guru, and good friend. While age and health made last year's trip very possibly our last, we remain in love with the city and the many friends we have made there over the years.

"First Spritz Is Free" by Kathleen González

"California! Welcome back!" Bepi sees me coming and puts the chips basket atop the glass counter. "Spritz Aperol?" he asks, but why? He knows that's what I come here for.

Spritz and a sense of coming home.

Bar Tiziano doesn't look like much: It's not an open-beamed gem from the fifteenth century; no copper pots hang over the oven, no spindly, spiny *cicchetti* peek out of the glass case. Instead, big windows light the bright interior, and a black and white photo on the wall shows a well-dressed American woman walking down the street while a man on a Vespa cranes his neck to ogle her. Tourists stream in to grab bottles of *acqua naturale* from the refrigerated case, and locals with their fluffy little dogs gesticulate with the hand not holding their drink.

I've known both Bepi and Claudio, the other long-time barista, since 1997 when I spent six weeks in the nearby Santi Apostoli neighborhood. One time we all went out for white pizza, but usually I just stop in for my first spritz upon returning to Venice. When I ask, "*Quanto le devo?*" Bepi rolls his eyes and walks away with my empty glass. Claudio turns up the corners of his mouth in a semi-smile. "For you . . .," they say and shrug.

And I'm addicted.

In Spring 1996, I traveled to Venice for the first time with nine of my students, my parents tagging along. Our tour bus had dropped us at Piazzale Roma, we crossed a couple bridges, then boarded the *vaporetto* up the Grand Canal. San Simione Piccolo's dazzling green dome winkled in the sun, and light bounced up onto my face from the waves. I saw the raspberry and burnt orange Hotel Principe. Inside my chest and belly, things rearranged themselves. My heart climbed up into my throat, and I couldn't look at the others in my group.

I hadn't just entered Venice. It had entered my blood and my consciousness.

I thought, "I have to live here some day."

I thought, "This is the most amazing place I've ever seen."

I thought no more thoughts because I was inundated with longing and awe instead.

We wandered, we got lost, we took refuge at a *trattoria* where I overindulged in espresso and tiramisu and became dizzy. My dad told the waiter that I'd be happy to work in the kitchen with him, so he rubbed his finger against my palm. Singers serenaded us in our gondolas, while we gaped at the palaces and mossy walls and watched little fish jump in the canals. We dead-ended at more canals than I can remember, but also I stood slack-jawed in the Basilica San Marco, engulfed in gold light. Little did I know that these few hours would signal such a shift in my life.

Being a teacher, I was free to return to Venice that summer for a wonderful two weeks. I rented a tiny, beamed room at Hotel Bernardi near Campo Santi Apostoli. Owners Leonardo and Teresa befriended me. From my room near the lobby, I'd hear another American woman testing out her rudimentary Italian with Santina, the front desk clerk, and I thought, "Maybe I should try that."

As a lone creature seeking connections, I returned daily to nearby Bar Lucciola, where the barista Alberto soon started explaining Venice to me.

"You see, in the afternoon this same guy comes here for his *tocai*. In Venice, in the afternoon we have the *ombra*, the little drink. Have you tried the spritz yet?" He set this bright red aperitif down in front of me, a smiling orange slice nestled at the bottom, a fat green olive speared on a stick. I wanted so much to like it—it was a gift from my first friend in Venice—but it was so bitter! I had been raised on candy and sugar, not biting red liquids. And yet spritz became the drink I equated with Venice, the first drink I always ordered, the drink to sip as I wrapped myself in Venice again each time I returned.

In the hot midday, I'd tuck my sundress around my legs and sit in a shady or breezy spot—the end of the Punta della Dogana, or the archways on the Rio de l'Alboro near San Moisé, or under the Pescheria arcades. On my final day, a gondolier left the *traghetto* to crouch down and ask my name. "What you writing?" he asked as he pointed to my journal. This was Max, whose chatty friendliness led to a longer conversation about gondoliers, which led to the idea for a book.

Or really, it was just an excuse to return to Venice the next year.

But here's where things became more complicated. Back home, I had a boyfriend I had spent ten years with. The last few years had been rough, and he didn't object to my separate vacation. So in 1997 I returned to Venice for six weeks to write the book that became *Free Gondola Ride*. Max introduced me to Stefano, his brother Giannino, Stevio, Sandro, Paulo, Luca, and others. I spent my days surrounded by men who gave me all the attention and compliments I hadn't been getting back home. "He want to try with you," Stefano would explain as one of the guys would take my hand. Paulo began giving me Italian lessons as he rowed the *traghetto* back and forth at Santa Sofia. I would hurry back to the little apartment I was renting from Leonardo's aunt, next to Hotel Bernardi, to record every tantalizing encounter with these men.

I fell deeper in love with the city.

But I also began to love myself, to see myself as deserving of more than I was getting from my boyfriend.

The next summer I returned to Venice a single woman. I believe that Venice gave me back myself.

My explorations of the city really began in earnest. Ca' Rezzonico, Ca' d'Oro, the Ghetto, the Museo Correr, all quenched my thirst for knowledge of Venice's roots. Eating *spaghetti al nero di seppie*, I got squid ink in my teeth. I sipped *fragolino*, spritz, and *sgroppino* after dinner. On the hottest nights, I'd walk in a circuit around the city—from Santi Apostoli to the Rialto to the Merceria to San Marco to Santo Stefano to San Luca to San Bartolomeo—drenching my head under the *campi* fountains and laughing as the water ran down my face and chest. I flirted with baristas but also walked Fondamente Nove in tears, wondering what I was doing there. After tasting all the flavors, I decided *stracciatella* was mine. I scratched my head at the Arsenale lions, scrunched up my nose at *grappa*, and wobbled while I tried to stand in the traghetto. Venice sparkled for me, the water changing its moods as often as I did, the streets pulling me to them and not allowing me to return to my apartment till everything had grown quiet.

Some days I felt like Katherine Hepburn in *Summertime*, longing to join with others, but afraid to commit, wanting to grab life but still healing from the end of my relationship. Venice brought me solace—just standing atop the Ponte Doná at Fondamente Nove, watching the sun illuminate the brick walls of San Michele, calmed my breathing. Just the sight of Venice's silhouette as I rode in on the Alilaguna from Marco Polo, and my heart raced again.

Venice offered its many selves to me: the quiet Accademia with paintings larger than billboards; the Biennale's varied pavilions and palaces I could peek into; Redentore where stars fell from the sky. I returned with friends for Carnevale, was chased by firemen with inflatable hammers, waited for the bathroom with a gorilla, caroused with the Four Gentlemen of Verona, and went to bed with confetti in my underwear.

This love affair lasted for years, with the peaks and valleys any relationship has. I shared Venice with friends, and I made new friends from Venice's inhabitants. I introduced my friends to spritzes, tried them at l'Olandese Volante, at Caffé Noir or Bar Rosso, at Muro, at Banco Giro, at Baffo, or always back at Bar Tiziano. I tried my spritz with Aperol, Campari, even Select. My gondoliers always welcomed me back, and if I were lucky I'd get a free ride back to moor the boat at night. Friends moved away, Alberto sold Bar Lucciola, I struggled to publish my book on the gondoliers.

My California life flourished, though, and I found a new man to share my life with. RJ supported my Venice obsession, helped me publish *Free Gondola Ride*, then helped me hatch a plan for a guidebook to Casanova's Venice. If my body couldn't be in Venice, well, my head could be, and writing about my favorite city fed my yearning. Now when I returned, I saw Venice differently: that cranberry colored palace wasn't just the one across from Marco Polo's house; it was the place where Casanova lived as Senator Bragadin's adopted son. This random street actually led to Casanova's grandmother's house, and this tiny courtyard provided the view from Casanova's apartment window.

Stefano, my faithful gondolier friend, said, "I think you know more about Venice than the people who live here all their life."

Venice provided the introduction to new friends—fellow bloggers, expats, my publisher, and the American woman who gave me my next book idea to explore the lives of Venetian women. Back home in California, I read dozens of books on this city, then returned with anecdotes on every third *palazzo* on the Grand Canal. I explored new neighborhoods besides Santi Apostoli, staying on the Lista di Spagna, near Campo Sant'Agostin, in Castello near Fondamente Nove, in the Frezzeria, or near Sant'Angelo Raffaele. I sang along with Furio Forieri at the *sagra* in Campo San Giacomo da l'Orio. I tried to get lost and found I still could if I left my well-worn habitual tracks. Now Venice gave me a sense of purpose.

Do the churches, palaces, cobbles, canals indeed have inherent beauty? Or do they have that beauty because I have invested them with it through memory and desire? Does Venice's attraction stem from my need for a haven, a paradise, an escape from the trap I was unable to extricate myself from? Perhaps this is true for my early days in Venice, in 1996 and 1997, when returning to the city felt like passing through a hidden door into an alternate universe where I found attention, eyes that found me beautiful, mouths that said so. Venice would forever be a safe anchorage for me because it was the place where I learned to love myself and learn that I deserved love. But now Venice is the vessel for my creative output, for friendships and community. She is my muse and the home of a big slice of my heart.

Max and Stefano and I have watched each other grow older, our hair grow silver, kids grow up, parents die. If the timing is right, they still give me a free gondola ride back to the mooring at Santa Sofia. Leonardo and Teresa's son is now helping to manage Hotel Bernardi. Bepi and Claudio still won't accept payment for that first spritz, and I keep returning, again and again, wondering what else this city will give me.

Biography

Kathleen Ann González has independently published four books, her first being Free Gondola Ride *about Venice's gondoliers, then a guidebook to Casanova sites in Venice titled* Seductive Venice: In Casanova's Footsteps, *followed by* A Beautiful Woman in Venice, *a collection of biographies. She also has essays in anthologies and periodicals, and three of her books have been published in Italy with Supernova Edizioni. Her research and ideas have also been used in a French documentary, other authors' books, and for the exhibit "Casanova: The Seduction of Europe." As a high school English teacher, she has won various awards and recognition for her work. Passionate about travel, González finds any excuse to hop on an airplane, particularly to Venice. Please visit KathleenAnnGonzalez.com for details about her work or follow her blog at seductivevenice.wordpress.com.*

"My First Spritz Was My Last Spritz" by Tony Green

My first spritz was my last spritz.

I never understood the fascination with this God awful, orange, pinky drink that is a mixture of either Aperol or Campari and Prosecco with an olive impaled on the end of a huge toothpick tossed in for further damage with the obvious intent to leave me with a terrible headache afterwards.

My first spritz was consumed in 1982.

I had just arrived in Venice, Italy, from the States where I was renovating houses in the Georgetown section of Washington D.C. to pay off my University of Maryland college bills. I was in the process of finishing off a Bachelor of Arts degree that I started a few years earlier in the '70s in Lafayette, Louisiana, home of the then-named University of Southwest Louisiana that had the prestigious honor of being voted the #1 party school in *Playboy Magazine.*

My Cajun studies were interrupted as I took off to Europe to search for my grandma in Aberdeen, Scotland. As I hitchhiked across Europe, I managed to stumble upon a country called Belgium where I settled into a fourteenth century building, living above a health food restaurant in the Gothic city of Brugges, Belgium (the "Venice of North Europe"). It began two years of painting in Brugges and playing rock n' roll with my group The Houserockers all around Flanders. A year of traveling throughout West Africa while being based in Accra, Ghana, rounded out my three year sabbatical from my BFA pursuits.

One of my Georgetown clients happened to be an English lady named Caroline Davidson who at one time was the governess for the old Venetian bloodline family of Marino and Rosella Zorzi. Marino was the head of the National Marciana Library (located in Piazza San Marco), which is one of the biggest and most important libraries in Italy. Rosella was a professor of American Literature at the Ca' Foscari University. Caroline suggested I contact the Zorzis about possible employment in Venice, as the couple were prone to help out young American students.

So I wrote them a letter.

Three months had passed and I had forgotten all about the idea of a Venetian getaway when a response arrived in the form of a letter stating that the Zorzis had just purchased a *palazzo* on the

Fondamente Nove, and would I be interested in helping them out with the renovation of the building in exchange for accommodations in the *palazzo*.

I thought about that for about three seconds and said, "Yes!"

Turns out it was the Palazzo Merati, that some people say was the residence where the infamous Venetian Giacomo Casanova resided and was eventually arrested.

And the situation got better/worse: the building was purchased together with a colorful character named Count Emile Targhetta Daudiffret Di Greoux who lived completely in the eighteenth century. Included in his repertoire was a costumed black manservant who traipsed around the highly decorated *palazzo* all day, ever responsive to the whims of the eccentric Count Targhetta.

I lasted but a few months in this bizarre atmosphere as in the end, I wouldn't go down for the Count!

So I left the Palazzo Merati adventure behind and started out on a three-year project of landscape painting in Venice while bouncing around from one cheap apartment to the next, accumulating a nice body of work and a solid group of Venetian friends.

Venice is an incredible place to be an old school landscape painter as it's 360 degrees of subject matter housed in 900 years of history. Subject matter was not a problem. Finding buyers for my paintings was. But somehow I managed to eke out a living from the profits of my painting sales. One of my early artistic associates was the notorious English painter Geoffrey Humphries whose legendary parties staged in his bohemian studio on the Giudecca were a great source of frolicking and of the meeting of new acquaintances, especially of the female persuasion. Geoffrey introduced me to a whole other side of Venice that most folks don't have the pleasure of experiencing.

I had to return to my New Orleans roots where as fate would have it, I met my latest girlfriend at the time and also my painting maestro, Auseklis Ozols, who hailed from the East European country of Latvia. Auseklis was a direct connection to the Renaissance as he studied with a guy, who studied with a guy, who studied with a guy, who had hands on information and the ability to raise my awareness to the beauty and wonders that surround us all.

I would study the fundamentals of painting with Auseklis for six months at the New Orleans Academy of Fine Arts then return to

Venice for the other six months with my girlfriend to put these valuable art lessons into practice. As I created a body of work, I had a steady stream of exhibitions of my Venetian paintings, including one-man shows in London, Switzerland, Venice, Holland, and New Orleans.

Life was good!

And it got even better as the money was rolling in and my painting technique improved.

Somehow living in a city with no cars, no crime, and no potholes encouraged my work habits that enabled me to reach higher artistic goals. And I'm still reaching.

I can remember one summer day walking through the *sestiere* of Dorsoduro when I abruptly stopped in front of this antique store to behold one of my paintings sitting there in the shop window for sale! So I entered and inquired to the owner about who was the author of this familiar self-creation. The shopkeeper proceeded to explain to me that the painting was the product of a long DECEASED American artist!

Caspita!

Morto!!

Upon hearing this dreadful news, I immediately whipped out my Louisiana driver's license, plunked it on top of the canvas, and invited this misinformed hustler to compare the two signatures.

PSYCHE!

Hey baby, you can't bamboozle a dude who was born in Naples, conceived in Venice (Hotel Regina), and raised in New Orleans!

But you know, one never gets bored walking around Venice as there's always something to discover and new things to do. A trip up the elevator of the Campanile of San Marco, for example, was always a treat not only for the incredible view it offered of the city and the lagoon but also because of the phone booth that was situated right under the huge and powerful Marangona bell. This beast would blast daily at 9 a.m., noon, 3 p.m, 6 p.m., and midnight. Therefore I would plan my international phone calls from the Campanile phone booth to back home at precisely 8:59 a.m. (which happened to be 2:59 a.m. New Orleans time), wait for the victim's sleepy response, and hold up the handset to let them bathe in the tonal glories of the Marangona!

Then there was the time I was invited with my Gypsy Jazz trio to perform at the Palazzo Pisani Moretta for their huge and overpriced carnival ball extravaganza. I had already given concerts at the Fondazione Cini, Ca' Foscari University, various festivals around Italy, and played at every jazz club in Venice.

The pay was great, and costumes were "de rigueur" for the patrons and the employees alike. But the party organizers doled out these leftover and embarrassing Little Lord Fauntleroy outfits to the lowly musicians. We had played but just one tune for the party patrons when we were given the cutthroat sign from the party planner. The next thing I knew this opulent, sixteenth century architectural masterpiece was submerged in hideous, ear splitting, and crappy disco music. I sought refuge in the upper floors where Harpo Marx took over my body and had me romping through the Pisani Moretti torturing the high-toned tourists with silly pranks and New Orleans style Mardi Gras mayhem.

Eventually though, the six months of back and forth between Venice and New Orleans got to be a bit schizophrenic, so I came back to Venice for just three months in the summer while building a career in New Orleans by painting murals and performing with my Tony Green & Gypsy Jazz ensemble. This is a music that is inspired by the late, great gypsy guitarist Django Reinhardt. The problem is that performing Gypsy Jazz in Italy is like being a hockey player in Bombay, India: there's no demand or appreciation for the music!

The intercontinental rhythm between New Orleans and Venezia was working out pretty well until Hurricane Katrina came along. The aftermath of this devastating storm blew me right back to Venice's waiting arms where I've set up shop ever since. I'm now a full time resident in the Jewish Ghetto where I exhibit my latest paintings at the Imaogars Gallery in the Ghetto Vecchio while my murals and large paintings are on permanent display at the Ristorante Upupa located in the Campo Gheto Novo. I maintain a vegetable garden on my *terrazzo* while keeping to a strict schedule of running over the many bridges of Venice and working out at Gymnos, which happens to exhibit my latest "conspiracy theory" etchings. I even ran the Venice Marathon back in 2009!

Unfortunately, I've witnessed the steady decline of culture in Italy as television, Hollywood, and the entertainment industry have succeeded in the dumbing down of the population.

But it's not the just the Italians who are the victims of the globalist's malevolent social engineering and failed educational system.

An American woman fresh off one of the cruise ships docked at the Tronchetto walked into my gallery in the Ghetto one morning. She parked herself in front of one of my large New Orleans paintings that depicted three women of color partying in the midst a second line parade.

"Gee, that's a pretty painting!" said the American tourist.

"Thank you!" said I. "It's called 'The Three Graces.'"

"Oh...." After a few moments of mental struggle the lady responded, "So why do they all have the same name?!"

Right...

After 36 years of living in La Serenissima, I've managed to carve out a healthy and focused lifestyle of exercise, eating well, gardening, painting, and practicing my guitar. And I look forward to another 36 years in Venice, but without the spritzes!

Biography

I maintain a gallery in the Ghetto Vechio four months out of the year, May, June, September and October, to exhibit my latest paintings. But the gallery is not just about paintings. It's a re-education center where I share pertinent information with people from all over the world to get them to think outside the box and help to wake them up from their trance caused by the electronic medication of the masses. It's sort of like a Jewish "Midrash" of discussion, learning, and sharing.

This type of alternative thinking culminated in a 47-minute film I made last year entitled "Tony in the Ghetto" that was advertised by one film critic as "a sugar coated truth bomb" ornamented with lots of live music, challenging information, and a few silly jokes. The film can easily be found on YouTube where you can also find twenty of my "Off Planet with Tony Green" podcasts that cover such diverse subjects as Chemtrails, the Federal Reserve Bank, and MKULTRA Mind Control.

All my films, interviews, paintings, and Gypsy Jazz performances can be found by visiting my website: tonygreen.net.

"A Passion for Venice" by Dianne Hales

More than three decades ago I descended into the darkness of Milan's grim train station and emerged hours later in a maritime Oz. In this fantasy world, half sea and half land, the streets ran with water, rows of crenellated *palazzi* soared above me, and seagulls swooped low over my head.

Appearing from nowhere, a *facchino* (porters abounded then) asked my hotel, grabbed my bag, and trundled off. I rushed to keep up, scrambling onto long wooden ramps above the *acqua alta* (high water) that lapped just beneath my feet. Walking on water, I would not have been surprised to sprout wings like Venice's emblematic lion and take to the air.

In that first vertiginous visit, La Serenissima literally brought me to my senses. I was alone but never felt that way. Sensations swept over me with every blink, sound, taste, scent, and touch. Each bend in a canal or turn of a calle (from the Latin for "path") revealed a new three-D pop-up stage set: Churches of brilliant white. Villas of pink and coral. Hump-backed bridges. Carnevale masks glittering in shop windows. Sleek black gondolas gliding by. Everything in constant movement, with reflections and shadows everywhere.

As a dutiful tourist, I trekked through cathedral-sized halls of paintings. My neck ached from constantly looking up. Artists with names as lyrical as their works—Tiepolo, Giorgione, Tintoretto, Tiziano—tugged my gaze into ever-ascending clouds. Massive battles raged across palatial walls. Milky-breasted goddesses and lusty gods pranced and preened. The Basilica of St. Mark gleamed with so many gold leaf mosaics that it seemed to glow from within.

One night I took myself to the opera at La Fenice, the historic theater that would burn to the ground in 1996. In its jewel-box interior, I thought of the countless others—lovers, voyagers, courtesans, dandies—who had sashayed through its vestibule to drench themselves in music and romance. The opera was Mozart's *Così fan tutte*, which loosely translates as "All Women Are Like That"—a phrase that pairs nicely with Venice's famous motto *"Siamo a Venezia"* ("We are in Venice"). Anything goes. No rules apply.

In a city brimming with tactile delights, I struggled to keep my hands to myself. I wanted to caress soft velvets, finger intricate laces, fondle delicate glassware. Venetians tolerated all these minor transgressions—but drew the line at fruit. When I dared to reach into a green grocer's stand and brazenly pluck an apple with my own hand, the horrified owner rushed to snatch it away. Knowing only a few shreds of Italian, I managed to comprehend that I could point. He would pick.

At times I simply followed my nose. Centuries of incense and candle smoke wafted from chapels. The heady whiff of chocolate lured me into confectionaries; streams of lavender and rose, into perfume shops selling tantalizing scents. Not every smell delighted. In early morning jogs along the Rialto, I felt that I was literally running with fishes. The stench of fetid water alerted me to many a canal's dead end.

On that first solitary trip, I ate at no fine restaurants. Instead, I lingered over a morning cappuccino or an afternoon *aperitivo* in the Piazza San Marco. At casual *trattorie* I devoured *risi e bisi* (rice and peas), *risotto al nero di sepia* (risotto in black squid ink), and whatever seasonal specialties the waiters proffered. When I grew hungry on my dawn-to-dusk ambulations, I stopped to sample the small plates called *cicchetti*.

With an undeniable stab of yearning, I watched love-struck couples riding in gondolas or walking hand-in-hand. I reminded myself of the advice of Peggy Guggenheim, who lived for decades among her modern art treasures on the Grand Canal. Never choose Venice for a honeymoon or romantic tryst, she cautioned. "To live in Venice or even to visit it means that you fall in love with the city itself. There is nothing left over in your heart for anyone else."

A few years later, pregnant with our first child, I took the risk and returned with my husband. Eagerly sampling Venice's romantic charms, we dined in candlelit *trattorie* deep in its warren of back streets. While I abstained from wine, the waiter poured an extra glass for the *Papa*-to-be and unfurled an extra napkin to protect my baby bump. Inevitably, we got lost in Venetian labyrinths—and kissed in the shadows. When we hired a gondola for the requisite moonlit cruise, the gondolier added lullabies to his repertoire.

Shopping for maternity clothes, I quickly learned that fashionable Venetian women disdain standard pregnancy apparel, which tends toward the dumpy and dowdy. A gaggle of sales clerks animatedly debated various options and recommended the style of the season: crisp, oversized shirts in a rainbow of colors. I bought one in bright lipstick pink that I kept for years simply for the happy memories of our Venetian Spring.

Over the next two decades, Bob and I returned to Venice only once. As we explored different regions of Italy, other ports and places held us in their thrall. Then we heard warnings from returning visitors: "Venice is ruined," they proclaimed. Massive cruise ships loom over San Marco. Hordes of tourists jam the streets. The museums and churches are packed. The stench is unbearable, the prices, astronomical. We stayed away.

About two years ago I began researching a new book: *La Passione: How Italy Seduced the World.* Of course, I would have to visit the city of seduction—and, of course, I insisted, we would have to go at Carnevale. And so we did—but not the Disneyfied Carnevale of elaborate costumes and expensive balls that draws tens of thousands of visitors. We arrived for the simpler, smaller, sweeter celebration held just before the official festivities in the working class neighborhood of Cannaregio, where the highest percentage of native Venetians lives.

There we watched a glorious parade along its canal—the oldest waterway in Venice—led by a silver sphere like a moon lassoed from the sky, with acrobats suspended in air, sky ballerinas unfurling streamers, and fire dancers juggling torches on gondolas. From booming loudspeakers, an announcer described the crowd as *veneziani fra veneziani* (Venetians among Venetians), celebrating their creativity, their dedication, and, most of all, their love for their city.

For one magical evening, we heard no languages other than Italian or Venetian. Children scampered in harlequin costumes. Women swirled in the velvet robes of another age. Men donned the long-beaked masks of plague doctors. Confetti fell like snowflakes. I began to appreciate fully the theory of a Russian psychoanalyst named Isaak Abrahamowitz, who contended that simply living in their perennially overheated sensory microclimate instilled "a permanent state of romantic excitement" in Venetians.

On our most recent trip to Venice, we succumbed to this seductive spell in high style. We stayed at the Hotel Cipriani, restored to its fabled splendor, in a suite overlooking the Grand Canal. The first night we ate in our room—the shutters flung open despite the winter chill so we could listen to the murmur of boats and waves. One morning we watched the reenactment of an ancient regatta from the balcony. Dozens of boats sailed past our windows, their rowers in costumes that ranged from nautical uniforms to harlequins to large yellow rats. Chants echoed along the canal. Bright banners fluttered in the air. We cheered, not for any particular boat, but for the spectacle itself. At night we walked under a canopy of tiny lights like stars snatched from the sky to dine at the lushly romantic Ristorante Quadri overlooking Piazza San Marco. As we headed back to our hotel, the moon glazed the lagoon in silvery light.

On this trip I also spent more time than ever with native Venetians. With my guide, the endlessly knowledgeable Cristina Gregorin, I talked with weavers in the last traditional silk mill in Venice and glassblowers on the island of Murano fashioning exquisite pieces of art with techniques handed down for centuries. In workshops throughout the city, I interviewed jewelers, woodworkers, ceramicists, and other craftspeople keeping alive Venice's oldest traditions.

Each interaction reminded me of an observation by the historian William Thayer, who described the Venetians as "magnificent by nature" a century ago as he wandered along the city's waterways, asking, "What poets dreamed these marvels? What romancers dwelt in these enchanted halls?"

While Casanova may be Venice's most infamous "romancer," the one who lives most vividly in my memory is an older gentleman with a white goatee and a jaunty beret whom I met during my first visit to Venice. One evening a chilly north wind had blown the tourists back to their hotels. Shrouded gondolas rocked in the lagoon. A full moon, white as Carrara marble, glided above Santa Maria della Salute.

The dapper gentleman approached me as I stood alone on a quay.

"*Che bella luna!*" I pointed at the moon, proudly unfurling some of the words I'd acquired in my stay.

"*Come Lei—anche Lei è bella!*" Like you—also lovely. I pretended not to understand the compliment.

"*Signorina, vorebbe un bicchiere di vino?*" (Would you like a glass of wine?) he asked, turning to face me.

"*Mi dispiace, Signore. Non parlo italiano. Mi dispiace.*" I apologized with the Italian phrase that translates as "I'm sorry" but literally means "it doesn't please me."

"Stop telling what is not pleasing to you," he said in a swift change to a curt and lightly accented English.

"But I ...."

"I know, I know. You don't mean to be rude. But I see a young woman, and I think, 'She should not be waiting alone for the moon to shine on her. She should be telling the moon to make her wishes come true.' Tell me, do you know how to ask for what you want in Italian?"

"*Voglio.*"

"*Beh!* I want! I want! That is for babies. No, you must speak like a lady, like a princess. You must say, 'It would be pleasing to me.' *Mi piacerebbe.*"

"*Mi piacerebbe,*" I replied, rolling the "r" as he had.

"*Sì! Sì! Ma che cosa Le piacerebbe?* What is it you would like, *bella donna della luna*—lovely lady of the moon?"

"I don't know. *Non lo so.*"

"Then you must find out. *La vita vola*: life flies. If you do not know what you want, you will never know where to look to find it."

"I would like—*mi piacerebbe*—to speak Italian, *parlare l'italiano.*"

"*Beh.* That's a start."

"And you—*e Lei?* What is your wish?"

"*Io? Mi sono invecchiato, ma ancora una volta mi piacerebbe baciare una bella donna alla luce della luna.*"

"I don't understand."

He moved very close. "I've become old, but I would like one more time to kiss a lovely lady in the moonlight."

For several seconds I watched the moon river shimmer on the canal. "*Siamo a Venezia,*" I thought to myself. And I did what it suddenly pleased me to do: I lifted my face to make his wish come true.

Biography

Dianne Hales is the author of Mona Lisa: A Life Discovered *and* La Bella Lingua: My Love Affair with Italian, the World's Most Enchanting Language, *a* New York Times *bestseller. The President of Italy awarded her the highest recognition the government can bestow on a foreigner: honorary knighthood, with the title of* Cavaliere del Ordine della Stella d'Italia *(Knight of the Order of the Star of Italy), for her contributions to the Italian language.*

*Dianne's newest book—*La Passione: How Italy Seduced the World—*will be published by Crown, an imprint of Penguin Random House, in April 2019. A widely published journalist, Dianne has also served as a contributing editor for* Parade, Ladies Home Journal, Working Mother, *and* American Health *and written for numerous national publications, including* The New York Times, Psychology Today, *and* The Washington Post.

Websites: dianpehales.com; becomingitalian.com; monalisabook.com

    *Blog: becomingitalianwordbyword.typepad.com
    *Facebook group: La Bella Lingua
    *Twitter: #dmhales

"Venice Between Poetry and Pragmatism"
by Judith Harris

Casanova, Goethe, Goldoni, Ruskin, Henry James: all have written gloriously about glorious Venice. Can the rest of us find words as eloquent, as poetic as theirs? Obviously not, but this cannot stop us. For Venice, composed of 118 islands and islets threaded through by 177 canals that are in turn crossed by 354 bridges, is now and will always be a poem writ in luminous reflections on its waters. To see it is like reading a sonnet: study it line by line, and gradually its meaning becomes ever more clear—or, rather, its multiple meanings, as, in the famous phrase of William Empson, speaking of the "seven layers of ambiguity" that can be read in Shakespeare's sonnets.

To see these layers is a challenge, even after my half-century of regular visits to Venice. The visitor must learn to look, which requires more than a generic love for the shimmering canals and elegant, venerable buildings. One should also take the time to pay attention to the details within the rich Venetian fabric of history.

As an example, from the home of friends where I once stayed for two weeks, I walked at least twice daily past a statue in the center of the Campo Santa Fosca. Only much later did I ask myself just who that statue represented. It turned out to be of the courageous monk Paolo Sarpi (1552 - 1623), who challenged the Church for its demanding the Venetians concede unconditional submission to Rome. The rift became so serious that Paul V of the Borghese family, elected pope in 1605, excommunicated Venice. The Church in Rome also accused Fra Sarpi of inspiring anti-papal pamphlets.

The result: in that very *piazza* in the beautiful Cannaregio neighborhood, at the instigation of the Pope, paid assassins attacked Sarpi with stilettos. Bleeding from no less than fifteen knife wounds, he was left for dead in that very Campo Santa Fosca. Miraculously he survived and lived ever after in a peaceful cloister until his death in 1623. From there he wrote a history of the Council of Trent, published in 1619 and widely translated, including into English, French, and German.

Knowing of this, that piazza can never be the same for me. It is haunting. And it is illuminating for what it tells us of the intellectual history of Venice.

Another example of what Venice is really about is the fascinating church, Santa Maria del Giglio, which I had blithely passed many times without grasping its significance. Looking more closely, I realized with surprise that, most curiously, its façade shows not a trace of Christian imagery. The church, which dates from the tenth century, was given an ornate marble baroque façade that celebrates, not a saint or two, but the mid-seventeenth century Venetian Admiral Antonio Barbaro, who, in fighting against the Ottoman Turks, destroyed no fewer than 84 of their ships. The Admiral, who died in 1689, bequeathed 30,000 ducats to rebuild the already ancient church in celebration of himself.

His statue thus stands in the center of the façade while, guarding its corners, are statues of his four brothers. Side panels illustrate various battles in which the Admiral had triumphed over the Ottomans including Split (Spalato to the Italians), Heraklion (Candia), and Zadar in Croatia. Other façade panels are dedicated to Padua and Rome, where the Admiral had served for a time as the Venetian ambassador to the Papal State. That map in stone amounts to a miniature tour of Rome.

Topping all this, like a cherry atop a cake, is a version in marble of the Barbaro family's bizarre coat of arms. Their crest, which shows only a big red circle on a grey background, is particularly unappetizing, for it represents an early Barbaro, Marco, who had chopped off the hand of a Saracen during a naval battle around the year 1125. With the blood from the hand, Marco Barbaro took his enemy's turban and drew, on it, a circle.

In the words of John Ruskin, that incredible church façade is so secular that it amounts to "insolent atheism."

A third example of seeking the significance behind the obvious are the over 600 well heads, many finely carved in marble, that decorate the *piazze*. The lagoon water could not be consumed, so, in the year 1322, the Venetians began construction of their first 50 wells. To do so they built, atop the layer of clay at the bottom of the lagoon, a series of very large cisterns in which rainwater was collected and then filtered through another layer of sand. From these cisterns the clean water was fed into the scattered wells. In times of drought Venetians actually purchased rainwater from neighboring towns and hauled it to refill their wells. All this became a triumph of both hydraulic engineering and, in the carvings of the well heads, of beauty.

If these examples speak for the glory centuries of Venice, its triumphs and problems, real change and a reverse of fortunes were to come in the nineteenth century. Napoleon's seizing the four ancient bronze horses of Venice marked the lagoon city's low point. The horses were returned with Napoleon's defeat in 1815, but not so the wealth that had permitted the construction of the great *palazzi* like the late Gothic Ca' d'Oro—the Golden House, so called for its gilded walls—and the Palazzo Barbaro itself, acquired by the Admiral's descendants in 1465.

After the Napoleonic era, Venice increasingly attracted artists, writers, the ultra-cultivated and the merely wealthy from all over Europe as well as the United States. Especially the Americans found Venice a soothing instance of decadence and pleasing contrast from the manufacturing cities of the US Northeast, like Boston. Finding it meant buying it—and the great double Palazzo Barbaro on the Grand Canal passed into the hands of the rich Bostonian merchant banker Daniel Curtis and his wife, who became the doyennes of Venetian society.

At that time the Venetians themselves were in deep trouble. Many were also in debt, for the Austrian rulers (ousted only in 1866) neglected the Venetian ports in preference to Trieste. At the same time the manufacturing revolution sweeping Northern Italy bypassed Venice for the better-connected Milan and Turin. So many jobs were lost that the Venetian population declined by one quarter in just a dozen years.

The one hundred or so aristocratic Venetian families sold off their *palazzi*, paintings, and possessions, one by one. The Curtises, who first rented the fifteenth century Palazzo Barbaro in 1880, purchased it in 1885 for the equivalent of around $16,000. (In 2017 its top two floors were sold for $2 million.) The Curtises found the *palazzo* (in reality a double *palazzo*) in terrible condition, and painstakingly and expensively restored it to its former glory. The interior of its *piano nobile* was painted by John Singer Sargent, who happened to be a Curtis cousin.

One by one the Venetian patricians lost their *palazzi*. The magnificent Palazzo Pisani, owned by the descendants of a famous eighteenth century doge, had to be sold off. An inventory of its paintings in 1809 mentioned Titian, Tintoretto, Veronese, Jacopo da Bassano, Lorenzo Lotto, Anthony Van Dyck, and Palma il Vecchio. The inventory, of course, was made because the paintings were being offered for sale. If so, there was a reason. Venice had been left "on the periphery," in the words of Venetian historian Adolfo Bernardello.

Another sign of the times: in 1810 the descendants of the Pisani doge sold off their collection of rare books and maps, several of which dating from the fifteenth century now belong to Stanford University. In 1815, British diarist Hester Lynch Thrale wrote that, "The ancient nobles, men and women, beg charity in the public streets. All mirth and gaiety are banished." Priests were reduced to selling their altars. She described a Venetian descendant of a doge, Mme. Foscarini, in the street holding out her hand for coins.

Venice tried to fight back. In 1840 a Venetian businessman planning to manufacture carpets and bolts of felt imported machinery from England. But because there was insufficient local consumption, within three years two hundred of his three hundred factory workers had to be fired, and 34,000 meters of unsold fabric were left to rot.

To encourage industry and give Venice an easier link than the gondola to the rest of Italy, the railroad bridge we take today was built from plans that began under the Austrians in 1836, to cover a distance of 3,547 meters. This was a part of what was only Italy's third railway line, and permission for construction came only in 1842. Historians describe the bridge construction, which was paid by the Austrians as well as the Venetians, as a "bottomless well." Still, by 1842 the link between Mestre and Milan was completed and the bridge into the lagoon city inaugurated in 1846 by the Emperor of Austria, the Archduke Karl Ferdinand. This fascinating and courageous adventure marked the first time that the lagoon city was physically linked to the Italian territory.

And what of today? During the twentieth century tourism revived the economy as do the craft products like Murano glass and Burano lace work. Outlying islands produced farm products like the artichoke known as the *carciofo violetto di Sant'Erasmo*. However, the number of farms has dropped notably from the 917 of 2007, while the fishing industry, once important, has dwindled sharply.

Meanwhile, the Porto Marghera became a petro-chemical center, these days highly contested for its polluting nature, which employs over 7,000. No one ignores the hordes of day trippers who rattle through the narrow lanes, still brought into Venice on abominably large cruise ships.

On the bright side the fresh news is that as of 2018 a new train line links Venice via Milan to Turin, with an increase in the speedy trains called Le Frecce. In addition, four times daily—and this is a first—fast trains go directly from the Santa Lucia station in the heart of Venice on to Mestre, Padua, Bologna, Florence, Roma Termini, Roma Tiburtina, and Napoli Centrale. Previously travelers had to change at Bologna.

Admittedly, this pragmatic footnote lacks the poetry and romance that characterize the Venice that so delights all of us. Still, if the lover of the arts dreams of the Venice of Ruskin and Henry James, of Sargent and Canova, of Vivaldi and Luigi Nono, not to mention the cartoonist Hugo Pratt, it is important to be able to get there to see it. And it is important that Venetians continue to mold glass, to make lace, to celebrate their Carnevale, and to glide under bridges in their gondolas.

i William Empson, *Seven Types of Ambiguity*, 1930, 1947, 1953. Prof. Empson taught English literature at Sheffield University and literally "revolutionized" the reading of poetry.
ii Bernadello, "Venezia 1830-1866, Iniziative economiche, accumulazione e investimenti di capitale," *Il Risorgimento*, 1, 2002 (Venice: Istituto Veneto di Scienze, Lettere ed Arti, 1996), 20. Among his other works is *La Prima ferrovia fra Venezia e Milano. Storia della Venezia Imperial regia privilegiata strada ferrata Ferdinandea Lombardo-Veneti* (1835-1852).
iii Bernardello, op. cit., 20.

Biography

Judith Harris, prize-winning author and freelance journalist based in Rome, Italy, was born in Lakewood, Ohio, and is a graduate of Northwestern University. She worked in Rome for six years as a cultural attaché to the US Embassy.

Returning to freelance journalism, over time her reports from Italy have appeared in Time *magazine,* the Wall Street Journal, ARTnews, *and Reuters Agency. For 25 years she conducted a biweekly broadcast on Italian culture for RAI International.*

At age seventeen she won her first journalism prize, and for her reporting on Italian terrorism for NBC TV she was included in the Peabody Award. She is currently the Italian correspondent for the online magazine www.i-italy.

She is the author of three books: Pompeii Awakened (I.B. Tauris), The Monster in the Closet *(American History Imprints), and* Evelina: A Victorian Heroine in Venice *(Fonthill Media). Her forthcoming book, just completed, is* REFLECTIONS from a Roman Lake. *Her full biography can be seen at judith-harris.com.*

"Venice, A Comfy Cocoon" by Mayumi Hayashi

I still remember the view I saw the first day I visited Venice, which will be forever etched in my memory. It was a view from the Rialto Bridge over the beautifully curved Grand Canal and the magnificent architecture on both shores. The view was romantic and nostalgic at the same time. The water was shining, reflecting the sunlight, and there were all kinds of boats—*vaporetti*, gondolas, motorboats—going up and down the canal. It was nothing like I had ever seen. I had already visited many different parts of the world and had been travelling in Italy for over a month by then....

"This is the most beautiful city I have ever visited!" I remember murmuring to a Venetian friend who took me there, and, to my surprise, it was a surprise to him!

"Oh, really?! What an honor!"

What? I think almost everybody would have the same impression as me.

It was sensational. It was moving. My heart was grabbed by the city ever since.

I had seen picturesque places. I had seen amazing architecture. But this?

It is a masterpiece of nature, architecture, art, and centuries and centuries of history.

I only stayed for thee days in Venice during my first visit. The rest of the time after I left the Rialto Bridge only intensified my admiration and longing for the Serenissima. I had little previous knowledge of the place as it was a spontaneous decision when the friend I met in Tuscany suggested accompanying him to his hometown. I didn't even know it consisted of tiny little islands. I didn't know there were no cars or bicycles allowed on them.

Part of the fascination came from the fact that it was completely opposite to the way things worked in Tokyo where I had lived until I decided to drop everything and travel around the world. Tokyo has everything. You can get pretty much anything at any time all year round. The transport network is efficient and sophisticated. Services are prompt, and you never have to wait for anything. Tokyo seems to be fixed about making life more convenient day by day when it is already so convenient to the point you can stop being a human being, so to speak.

When I saw a middle-aged woman open a little wooden door in one of the alleys in the Rialto area, I was bewildered to know there are people actually living in Venice. It seemed too magical and detached from reality for people to be living in this environment. And I knew, from that moment, I had to try and live in this city. I was dying to find out what it was like to live there. Just like her, I'd like to own my own key to the door to one of these centuries-old buildings tucked in a little alley.

It wasn't easy and took a few turns. It also took several months of living in Mestre, the rather dull city on the other side of the Libertà bridge that connects Venice to *terraferma*, the mainland, before the dream came true. Finally, I found a perfect housemate and a gorgeous little flat facing a spacious and luminous square called Campo San Polo. When I obtained the keys to the building door, I was so proud! I used to open the door very slowly so that people could witness. They must be surprised to see that somebody actually lives in this place, like I had been that day! Actually, it wasn't very simple opening the door as most of the doors in Venice are a bit tilted due to the subsidence and you need a little trick. In my case, I had to hold the door slightly upwards as I inserted the key and pulled it towards me once before pushing it to open. My flatmate/landlord didn't even notice; she did all the sequence automatically, and she was amused to hear I struggled.

So, I lived in Venice from 2002 to 2012.

My life there at the beginning was like Alice in Wonderland.

I loved being lost in the narrow alleyways and finding precious little *campi* (squares) and hidden groceries and general stores for the locals. I loved it even more when I stopped being lost in this seemingly unfathomable labyrinth. Asking people for directions did not really help because the responders are either tourists who did not have a clue where they were themselves or the locals who were so sick of being asked that they would give you bare minimum information, if any. It is amazing and gratifying, though, after about three months of exploring various obscure alleys, you start to have some idea of the whole picture. Venice is a sort of place where a map doesn't help if it is a size you can hold with your two hands.

Google Maps used to point to my house in the middle of a canal in those days.

When you start to go around at least the area you live in without getting lost, you feel like you're one of the locals. You avoid the main alley that tourists stick to and stride the back alley that runs parallel to the main one. You know which route has fewer bridges to cross and which route has less area under water during *acqua alta*.

Oh, I thoroughly enjoyed the inconvenience of the Venetian life!

There are no cars on the island, so you always have to walk. There are boats—*vaporetti* (waterbuses) and *motoscafi* (water taxis), but *vaporetti* run only on wide canals so you often have to walk a good distance from the nearest stop and they were usually very crowded and expensive, even with special discounts for the residents. Taxis are out of the question, as they have the starting fare of 50 euros. However tired you may be, however drunk you may be, however big your shopping may be, you have to walk. Up and down the bridges.

Places were not always open. Whether they were government offices or privately-owned shops. They were closed for lunch, siesta, coffee, or just because they felt like it. Of course, they were closed on Sundays, bank holidays, and Monday mornings or sometimes all day on Monday. I don't know how many times I walked all the way across the island just to find the place I was going to was closed.

Acqua alta. With the combination of the tide and the weather, the water level rises and floods various parts of the city. In the morning of *acqua alta*, there is a siren that goes off, and judging from the length and the pitch of the siren you know how high the water will rise, and decide whether you need to take wellies with you that day or leave home earlier so you won't get caught by high water.

The usual amusement and entertainment that you would find easily in other ordinary cities was hard to reach. For big cinemas where you could see films in original languages, an amusement park, or any sports facilities, you would have to travel out to the mainland.

You might think I am being negative about the life in Venice. Quite contrarily, I loved every single element of the inconvenience. Compared to life in Tokyo, I felt I was actually living! I had to be resourceful, had to calculate timing, I had to organize myself a bit better. To me, it was a life probably similar to the way it was 30 years ago. I loved the life where you'd go down for a quick espresso in the tiny coffee place, stroll in the historical market to get fresh veggies, visit the favorite butcher for meat and the delicatessen for cheese, instead of just finishing all the shopping at one time in a huge supermarket or shopping mall. See and greet the usual faces en route and in the shops. Venice taught me how to live a daily life the way I wanted it to be.

Because there are no cars and everyone walks, the nightlife in Venice has its own character. It is dangerous in a way, because you cannot make an excuse like, "Well, I'm driving today." In the late afternoon, people in Venice are drawn to a drink of the same color as the sky at dusk. An orange cocktail called spritz is as popular as sushi in Japan and Vegemite in Australia. "*Uno spritz?*" is almost the same thing as saying "hi." You cannot avoid saying it if you bump into a familiar face on a street. Today it is a popular drink everywhere in Europe, but it all started in Venice. Strange because spritz does not taste the same when you drink it in any other city. With the same ingredients, it still tastes differently when you drink it standing in a narrow alley, eyeing the water in a canal, hearing nothing but boats and Venetian dialect. They say noises affect your taste buds. Maybe it has to be in the same environment without traffic noise to appreciate the same taste.

It was an inexpensive drink. When somebody said they wanted to have a Bellini, I knew they were tourists. Locals don't drink the cocktail that costs 12 euros a glass unless they are paid for. Locals drink spritz, the cocktail of Prosecco (or white wine), Aperol (or Campari) and fizzy water, that costs 2 to 2.50 euros a glass. That is why it was a great, easy drink to start an evening that scarcely stopped after "*uno spritz*" but rather that of many spritz and god knows what else. "*Ultimo* (last) *spritz*" was a famous phrase for just an opener for the second leg of the evening. "So, what? You are not driving tonight, are you? You don't have to worry about the last train to catch or anything."

Because you walk everywhere and everyone else does the same, you run across people you just met at a bar the night before on your way to work. In other cities, maybe you never see them again. Here in this city, you bump into them all the time! Before you notice you keep saying "*Ciao! Come va?*" every three seconds to people who you pass by. Thus, a sense of community grows quickly. The sense of community of the ones who live in this odd city. The sensation you can only share with people who have experienced it. It feels like it exists somewhere between the past and the present. Living in Venice is like living in a dream. You know it is not a real life. You know you have to get back to real life some time, but it is hard to do so. It is so cosy so you want to just forget about real life and stay there as long as possible. It is like a hidden pocket of the world. The world forgets about Venice until it is a holiday time or a start of the film festival, and Venice forgets about the world, too, as everything that happens beyond the lagoon seems so far away and detached. The passage of time seems to go very differently, and the discrepancy only grows with time.

In my case, I stayed in this comfy dreamlike cocoon for ten years, during which I met my husband. He was a dweller of the alluring cocoon, too. He is English but was a fully and widely accepted citizen of Venice. He understood more than anyone, in my opinion, the way of life and true beauty of Venice. He was the only Englishman who spoke Venetian. When I met him and started to live with him, I realized I could leave Venice finally. Even after I parted with the city physically, I would be living with a piece of it with me all through my life. When we see our beloved city of Venice in a film or advertising, I know we are feeling the same thing, the feeling that you cannot possibly express with words, and it is good that, between us, we don't need to.

We married in Palazzo Cavalli, the sixteenth century architecture that serves as the city hall of Venice. It was a beautiful civil wedding surrounded by close friends and family. Palazzo Cavalli is one of the striking palaces I saw from the top of the Rialto Bridge that day. Who could have imagined that I would be passing under the bridge in a gondola with my father next to me to get to the shore where my groom and friends awaited. It is true Venice is a magical place. At least, it was for me.

Biography

Mayumi Hayashi enjoys her European life in Barcelona with her English husband she met in Venice. She grew up in a small town in Japan and studied English in Australia. She was an English teacher in Japan before moving to Toulouse to learn French. Mayumi loves people and languages. Currently works as an interpreter and tour guide.

"What If the Doge Were Female?" by Mary Hoffman

My fascination with Venice is a subset of my fascination with Italy. That began when I was fourteen and was consolidated by a month in Florence when I was nineteen. But it wasn't until I had teenage daughters myself that I first visited Venice.

And it was only for a day.

We were staying in Desanzano near Lake Garda and discovered we could get to Venice by train, so why not? It wasn't the best day, being somewhat overcast, and I had a raging toothache, but we duly trooped out of the railway station and crossed the first bridge and followed the black arrows on yellow signs to San Marco.

Of course, we should have anticipated that the main thing the girls wanted to do was ride in a gondola, so we went down to the Piazzetta to negotiate. The ride cost rather more than five people's train tickets from Desanzano to Venice–return. And it was a psychotherapist's hour, a scant 50 minutes.

I began to scrutinize the gondolier. For that money he really should have been a sort of Greek god. Instead he was middle-aged, portly, balding. He was friendly enough and competent, in that sort of tour guide manner, knowing the main facts and following the same route and routine every trip.

I'm not sure if I recognized that was a "light bulb moment," but I certainly fell into a reverie in which I asked myself a series of questions; and that's how books often begin for me.

• How could you ensure all gondoliers were young and beautiful? Have them chosen by a woman.

• What woman would have that power? The ruler of the city.

• But Venice was ruled by a man, the Doge. What does that mean? It's dialect for duke.

• What is the Italian for duke? *Duca*.

• And the feminine of *duca*? *Duchessa*.

• Since Venice never had a *duchessa*, how could you make this happen? Set it in an alternative version of the city, in a parallel dimension.

Five years later, holidaying on the Lido with my husband and just the youngest daughter, I thought about this series of questions and answers again and found that in the meantime, the *Duchessa* of a parallel-world version of Venice had matured somewhere at the back of my mind into a fully-fledged character, called Silvia.

Intrigued to meet her, I started planning a novel initially called *Where Beauty Wears a Mask*. The city would be called Bellezza, the Italian for "beauty," and the action would take place in the sixteenth century. It would be ruled by an elected *Duchessa*, who was as politically ruthless as she was beautiful. Choosing gondoliers was a small perk of the job. But she definitely did it and made sure that they were as good-looking as ours was not. They could start at fifteen and were compulsorily retired at 25 with a generous pension. She would choose the best-looking to become her lovers.

But the story still needed something: a twenty-first century character through whose eyes we could view this alternative Venice. And so was born Lucien Mullholland, a fifteen-year-old suffering from brain cancer. Then I had to get him four hundred years back and a dimension away from his home in north London. So the science (or magic) of *stravagation* was invented and the book series name, "*Stravaganza*," born.

As you can imagine, there was much planning and plotting and world-building before I was ready to start writing the first book. And Lucien needed a guide to this different world, a girl a month or two older than him. I suddenly realized I could make her someone who wanted to be a gondolier but was barred by her gender. When Lucien first meets her, she has hidden all night in the city (she comes from one of the lagoon islands) and is dressed as a boy, so that she can apply at the school for gondoliers, *mandoliers* as they are known in Bellezza. Because of a misunderstanding, the *Duchessa* chooses Lucien.

Since the girl was Lucien's guide, I called her Arianna, the Italian equivalent of Ariadne, who led Theseus through the labyrinth. She is coming up to her sixteenth birthday, when she will have to start wearing a mask, as all unmarried women over sixteen must in Bellezza.

Masks, gondoliers, all the well-worn tropes of a Venetian story, but I wanted to use them in fresh ways. In the end, the first book was called *City of Masks* and was published in 2002 by Bloomsbury. The *Stravaganza* sequence ran to six books, each one set in a different Italian city transposed to the alternative country of Talia. The last book, *City of Swords*, set in a version of Lucca, was published in 2012.

But there continued to be scenes set in Bellezza, because that's where it all began. And although I intended each book to have different characters, there were five from *City of Masks* who insisted on going forward into the other books in the series: the *Duchessa* (of course!), Rodolfo her lover and Lucien's mentor, Lucien himself, Arianna, and Dr. William Dethridge, a sixteenth-century Englishman and alchemist, who invented the art of *stravagation*.

Dr. Dethridge was based on the real life historical character of John Dee, who was Elizabeth the First's personal astrologer and was also a mathematician, calendarist, and alchemist. Rodolfo turns out to have a strong personal link to Arianna. He was one of the handsome *mandoliers* that Silvia took to her bed but is now a powerful magician and a "*stravagante*," as these travellers between worlds are known.

The *Duchessa* is incredibly vain and uses young body doubles for any important ceremony, impersonations it is easy to carry off, since, as an unmarried woman, she always wears a mask in public. We discover this early on in a chapter called "The Marriage with the Sea," which inverts the well-known ritual in which the Doge casts a ring into the lagoon on Ascension Day.

In Bellezza it goes like this:

"At the climax of silver trumpets, two young priests reverently lowered the *Duchessa* into the sea from a special platform. Her beautiful dress floated around her as she sank gently, the priests' shoulder muscles bulging with the strain of keeping the ceremony slow and dignified.

As soon as the water lapped the top of the *Duchessa's* thighs, a loud cry of "*Sposati!*" went up from all the watchers. Drums and trumpets were sounded and everyone waved and cheered, as the *Duchessa* was lifted out of the water again and surrounded by her women. For a split second everyone saw her youthful form as the thin wet dress clung to her. The dress would never be worn again."

Only of course it wasn't the *Duchessa* they saw but one of her body doubles. "They all think I have the figure of a girl—and I do. What's her name this time?" asks Silvia when the wet and shivering girl is returned to the cabin inside the Barcone.

Venice is the sort of place where it feels as if anything might happen, and this was helpful for a book of fantasy, where magic and science were in interplay. It was also important to me that the city, Bellezza, should be a character in the novel in its own right. Bellezza and the Bellezzans love a good party and will have one at the drop of a hat.

They are also completely hooked on tradition and superstition. Their religion is goddess-based, and they frequently make the sign of the *manus fortunae*—the Hand of Fortune. "He made the sign that lagooners use for luck—touching the thumb of the right hand to the little finger and placing the middle fingers first on brow and then on breast."

We soon learn that the sign signifies the unity of the circle and the figures of the goddess, her consort, and son, the sacred trinity of the lagoon. Bellezzans exclaim "*Dia!*" which means "Goddess!" but it is their rituals and superstitious beliefs that underlie their way of life rather than theology or doctrine. And they hedge their bets by still building great churches, so they are a mixture of pagan and Christian.

The islands of the lagoon feature too, though their names have been distorted—everything in Talia is like something from our world that has been reflected in a distorting mirror. Arianna is from Torrone (= Torcello), where her father is the curator of the cathedral museum there. Her maternal grandparents live in Burlesca (= Burano), where they have the only white house among the multi-colored ones of their neighbors. Her grandmother makes lace, and her grandfather is a master patissier.

More familiar tropes but with a twist. For example, in a chapter called "The Language of Lace" Arianna's grandmother is able to warn the *Duchessa* of a planned assassination attempt by sending her a piece of lacework with a coded message in it.

Arianna's older brothers, two fishermen, live in a cottage on Merlino (= Murano), which is known for its glass-making. There is a glass museum there, much more interesting than the real life one on Murano, in which there is a room dedicated to the celebrated but anonymous Glass Master of the fifteenth century. On display is an exquisite glass mask, whose story Arianna tells Lucien.

The Glass Master made one like that for a Duchessa of a hundred years earlier, for her to wear at Carnival. She is dancing with the young Prince Ferrando di Chimici in the main square of the city when she trips and falls and the glass mask shatters, wounding her face. Courtiers rush to her side, convinced she has been the victim of an assassination attempt (there is a lot about assassination in this book), but Ferrando is innocent.

No one ever sees that *Duchessa's* face again; she always wears a mask and brings in the law that all unmarried women over sixteen must do so. She gets the Glass Master to make a replica of the mask that robbed her of her beauty; he dies the next day and Ferrando soon afterwards. All *Duchesse* are ruthless.

I don't have a place of my own in Venice. But I have a friend who does, and I've been lucky enough to stay with her and in other places many times over the years since that first disappointing gondolier. One memorable trip was a Bloomsbury sales conference, which involved staying at the Danieli, giving a talk and a guided tour to Bellezza, attending a masked ball, and having breakfast with novelist Barbara Trapido.

Every minute was glorious, but Bloomsbury CEO Nigel Newton was so shocked by the bill that the sales conference in the following year was held in Eastbourne.

My favorite *sestiere* was always Cannaregio, and indeed Lucien and Arianna have their first proper conversation in the Campiello de l'Anconeta in a caffè near a boarded-up theatre. This is the Teatro Italia, whose air of faded grandeur I loved for decades. It is now a Despar supermarket. Indeed, Cannaregio is getting more crowded and is not as I remember it when I had a holiday there as a local, shopping in a now-closed delicatessen and in the street market, which is still there.

But the last time I was in the city was for a literary festival, and all speakers were put up at a very smart hotel in the Giudecca. It had a large garden, full of spring flowers and the occasional rabbit. I was beguiled by the tranquility of the Giudecca and will return there, I hope.

Venice isn't the Italian city I know best (that is Florence) or even the one where I feel I most belong (that is Siena, in the Valdimontone *contrada*, where I'm sure I have lived in an earlier life). But Venice is the one that triggered six novels, which have been translated into over 30 languages. So it has a very special place in my imagination.

Biography

Mary Hoffman's Stravaganza sequence was published by Bloomsbury from 2002-12.

City of Masks *(Venice)*
City of Stars *(Siena)*
City of Flowers *(Florence)*
City of Secrets *(Padua)*
City of Ships *(Ravenna)*
City of Swords *(Lucca)*

"Finding Titian's House" by Frederick Ilchman

In October of 1996, I moved into an apartment on the Fondamenta dei Sartori, Cannaregio 4839, midway between Campo Santi Apostoli and the Gesuiti. I was beginning a Ph.D. dissertation on Jacopo Tintoretto in the 1550s, the period leading up to his magnificent paintings for the church of the Madonna dell'Orto. That church, which also contained the artist's tomb, was only a fifteen-minute walk from my flat. I took a long time to get my bearings in Venice's libraries and archives, frustrated by their limited opening hours and convoluted regulations. Therefore in those early months, I spent most of my days seeking out in person paintings from Tintoretto's era in museums and churches, and most of my evenings browsing books on my shelf. Nearly everything I saw or read was new to me.

A favorite volume was the stout red guidebook *Venezia*, published by the Touring Club Italiano. The third edition, from 1985, featured the marvelous section up front of diagrams of all the buildings on both banks of the Grand Canal, a precious resource for trips on the number 1 *vaporetto* from Piazzale Roma to Arsenale and back again. But the dense text of the guidebook contained far greater secrets. I followed the suggested itineraries, learning much about the historic structures and art treasures of many neighborhoods. But I was most fascinated by the index in tiny print at the back, with its hundreds of entries. In those first weeks, I tried to visit as many as possible of the churches listed, or call up in my mind the architects or styles of the long column of named *palazzi*. A couple of months into my stay, I was reading in bed around midnight. I found myself looking up again in the index the page for Tintoretto's house (a private home whose location on the Fondamenta dei Mori I knew well, having stood in front of it several times). To my surprise, on page 784, just under "Casa di Jacopo Tintoretto," I discovered an entry for "Casa di Tiziano," and was directed to page 554. I hadn't remembered that Titian's house was still standing. Finding the correct page, I read that the building was constructed in 1527 and that the painter would have originally enjoyed a view over the northern lagoon, before later construction occurred. It made sense to me that the great sunsets and misty landscapes in Titian's later *poesie* had been witnessed from that very spot. I was further astonished to see that the house number was listed as well (N. 5182-83). Noting that these numerals were not much higher than that of my building—and in fact only one bridge away—I immediately changed from pajamas to warm clothes and an overcoat, and set off.

A few minutes later, I was standing outside of Titian's house, in a totally modest corner of the city. I gingerly touched the *intonacco* on the building's exterior and gazed up at the dark windows of the *piano nobile*. I shivered when I realized that some of the greatest canvas paintings in the history of art were created in that unassuming building. And that until the old painter's death in 1576, the upstart Tintoretto would have been kept on his toes by the works emerging from that studio.

I was pleased with discovering at a crazy hour something so powerful about the Venice I was researching, a building hidden and in plain sight at the same time. A final, more sobering thought was that Titian's home would always be a closed door to me. That cold evening, I was already deeply in love with Venice. Starting with my first visit in 1986, I had been in awe of the city. On a later sojourn, I resolved to learn everything I could about it, knowing that I would never unravel all its mysteries. What really hooked me, however, was learning that select others shared my passion.

Venetophiles embrace many aspects of the city and its culture, putting a positive spin on even the mixed or mediocre. We are enthusiastic about *la Serenissima* to a quixotic extent, and many of us dedicate our lives to keeping Venice an intact and beguiling place. Often hopeless romantics, we can be very generous to the city and to those who love it. One of the greatest gifts is to introduce others to the magic of Venice, and I recall with great fondness Mitzi and George Stein, residents near the Redentore, who owned for two decades the Giudecca's second-best *altana*, but left Venice and this earth far too soon. Those smitten by Venice love to make discoveries. Our bond to the city is strengthened whenever we find a new cozy *osteria*, a quirky shop, a more lovely painting by Giovanni Bellini, or meet for the first time another fan of our favorite city.

My friends and I have been delighted to find out, for example, that the witty observations and anecdotes that pepper Jan Morris's classic travelogue *Venice* (1960) are really true. Indeed her stories and situations play out again and again in our experience, decades later. And we love to be surprised in Venice, and surprised by Venice. To have our hierarchies reordered. I remember just how suave I felt in the spring of 1997, standing at the top of the Rialto Bridge at dusk with a pleasant young woman. We were gazing toward the Fondaco dei Tedeschi, and I was trying to impress my date by discussing what it must have felt like to the Venetians, and specifically the merchants in the Rialto markets just to our left, to have heard the news in 1453 of the conquest of Constantinople by the Ottoman Turks.

Of course, we were in Venice, and I shouldn't have been so cocky in my narration. As we stood there, suddenly I was totally surprised myself, though admittedly not by something as earth-shattering as the fall of Byzantium. But surprised I was. Directly underneath us silently emerged the sleek prow of a gondola. But this boat wasn't laden with tourists; the seats were empty. Rather, the gondola was covered by dozens of tea lights, candles within little jars, all lit. Better still, the gondolier was very young with flowing hair. And barefoot. He was clearly going to pick up *his* date. I could only stare.

That evening I learned it was wise not to feel smug about anything in Venice, or consider oneself an expert. You could never know it all. Whistler admitted that he found the city too challenging to sketch because there was always "something still better round the corner." (I learned both this quotation and its essential truth thanks to Eric Denker's brilliant 2003 exhibition *Whistler and His Circle in Venice*.) There is always another corner to discover. On my very last day as an intern at the Peggy Guggenheim Collection in November of 1992, I turned left instead of right, returning to my tiny room on Campo Do Pozzi—and I discovered a neighborhood entirely new to me in Castello. And despite years of study, and three or four trips to Venice in a good year, I am always learning. Walking systematically the *calli* of Casanova took me through a completely different city than that of Tintoretto and Titian, thanks to Kathleen González's guidebook *Casanova's Venice*. Not only when standing on a *traghetto* does Venice keep us off balance.

How to repay my gratitude for years of astonishment? The American organization Save Venice, dedicated to the preservation of art and architecture throughout the city, both grounds me and allows me to give something back to the place I love so much. Since 1999,

I have held a wide range of positions in Save Venice, from volunteer to paid intern ("art history fellow") to the Executive Committee of the Boston Chapter to the national Board of Directors and now finally to its Chairman. The organization has contributed far more to me and my family than I could ever give to it. Often through the restorations, I have discovered major works I had never heard of (e.g. the canvases by Diziani in San Silvestro's Scuola del Vin), or passed by without paying sufficient attention, such as the Sotoportego di Corte Novo near San Francesco della Vigna. Other projects have rehabilitated unsung masterpieces, even by famous artists, such as Tintoretto's altarpiece from San Marziale. Save Venice's new office, and its marvelous Rosand Library and Study Center, with books available for consultation by appointment, offers a new and welcoming facility for students and scholars of Venetian art at any level. And we make sure that financial donations are wisely used in our goal to preserve artistic treasures for future generations.

To my delight, I continue to meet fellow Venetophiles, even as I continue to be surprised by Venice. Just two summers ago, researching the art of Casanova's time, I met a charming woman at a party, who soon included me at one of her dinners. You'll surely guess the location: Titian's house.

Biography

As a specialist in the art of Renaissance Venice, Frederick Ilchman was appointed Chair, Art of Europe at the Museum of Fine Arts, Boston, in 2014. He is also the Mrs. Russell W. Baker Curator of Paintings, a position he has held since 2009. He joined the MFA in 2001 as Assistant Curator of Paintings. He holds an A.B. from Princeton University and a Ph.D. from Columbia University, both in art history. Frederick has curated or co-curated such exhibitions as Titian, Tintoretto, Veronese: Rivals in Renaissance Venice (MFA and Musée du Louvre, 2009), Goya: Order and Disorder (MFA, 2014), Casanova's Europe (Kimbell Art Museum, Fine Arts Museums of San Francisco, and MFA 2017), and Tintoretto: Painter of Renaissance Venice (Palazzo Ducale and National Gallery of Art, Washington, 2018). He is also the national Chairman of Save Venice Inc., the largest private committee devoted to art conservation in Venice.

"The Day Job" by Philip Gwynne Jones

Sometimes you really have to want to live in this city.

The early start never gets much easier. It certainly isn't on the first school day of the new year. Our *calle* is almost deserted at this hour. Almost, that is, except for an elderly neighbor, slowly making her way home after an early morning *passeggiata* in near-darkness. She stops and asks, as she always does, where on earth I'm going to so early in the morning. I tell her, as I always do, that I teach at a school in Castello and that we have to start at 8:00. She shakes her head, "*Mamma mia,*" and continues her way along the *calle*. We will have the same conversation tomorrow morning. And the morning after. And, I expect, for as long as we both continue to live here.

The *fondamenta* outside the railway station is as quiet as it ever gets, the statue of the Madonna eerily silhouetted in the half-light. I make my way to the Line 2 stop. The *vaporetto*, as it always is at this hour, is jammed full of people. Not tourists, but rather people making their way to work, the majority of them catching the boat from Piazzale Roma after commuting from the mainland. The *marinaio* is crying "*Avanti in cabina*" time and time again, but there's more than a touch of tiredness in his voice. If we could, we would.

Then I notice that the outside seats at the front are still free. It's cold, properly cold, and nobody in their right mind would want to sit there without even their fellow passengers to provide a modicum of shelter. Still, it's a seat, and given that I have six hours on my feet this morning in front of classes of differing grades of delightfulness, I decide to go for it. I squeeze my way through the crowd and sit down, turning up the collar of my coat and pulling my hat down against the freezing air.

The canal is quiet at this hour, its surface undisturbed by gondolas, *traghetti*, or water taxis. I see a puff of cigarette smoke as we pass a transport boat, the captain keeping one hand on the wheel as he nonchalantly smokes with the other.

We pass the Casinò at San Marcuola, with its gnomic advertising slogan "Stop where emotion starts" which manages to be both amusing and irritating in equal measure. Then on past San Stae, lonely in the half-light, the statues on its façade gazing sightlessly out. Past the Rialto Market, where the fishmongers are already setting up their stalls for the day.

The *Fondaco dei Tedeschi*, once the Post Office and now a luxury shopping mall, is, as it always seems to be, lit up like a Christmas tree. Then the boat slides under the Rialto Bridge and towards the jetty where everyone disembarks. The sky is clearing now, no longer a deep midnight blue but a dull grey reflected in the color of the water.

Passarelle, elevated walkways, have been placed around the city in expectation of *acqua alta,* but, although water is lapping over the edge of the canal and on to the *fondamenta*, there is no serious high water predicted. No sirens have sounded, no warning texts have been received. There will be no need for rubber boots this morning.

I walk through to Campo San Bartolomeo, with its statue of a jovial, smiling Carlo Goldoni striding forth. Then I look in the window of the adjacent *farmacia*. The LED sign in its window is switched off, but I know what it would say. The *farmacia* has been displaying the population of the *centro storico* in its window for years now. When we arrived, not even six years ago, the figure was slightly less than 60 thousand. Now, it is not even 55 thousand. Every day, I pass by here, and every day I have the same thought: *For just how much longer can this city continue to be viable?* I glance up at Carlo Goldoni and wonder just what he has to smile about.

I pass under the *sotoportego*, where everybody slows their stride as the complete lack of lighting makes it difficult to see anything at all in the early morning light. Then over the bridge and along Salizada San Lio. The city is coming alive now. A few coffee bars are open, street sweepers are in action, and refuse collectors make their way from house to house. Some of the more enthusiastic students are already on their way to school.

I cross over the bridge to Campo Santa Maria Formosa and stop outside the small bar at the side of the canal that, legend has it, once served as an emergency mortuary. It will always be "the coffee shop of death" to me. The owner sees me peering in, shakes his head and taps at his watch. Still only 7:30. He won't be opening until 8:00. My regular coffee bar, on the other side of the *campo*, is, I know, closed in this quiet month of January, the staff taking a well-deserved break after New Year, in readiness for the chaos of Carnevale.

No matter. There's one remaining bar on my route that is always open at this hour. A welcome wave of heat hits me as I enter. I lay my hat on the counter. The barman nods at me.

"*Macchiatone?*"

"*Sí.*"

It's not a bar that I use often enough to have progressed to first name terms, let alone a cosy chat with the staff, but they still remember what I drink. A quirky little place, decoration provided by old record sleeves hanging from the ceiling. There is, as ever, the smell of warm brioche. And, as ever, I ignore it. I never feel like eating at this time in the morning. In two hours time I will regret this. I always do. Warmth is flooding back into me now. The heat of the coffee hits the back of my throat just before the blessed punch of the caffeine reaches my brain. I close my eyes and sigh. I feel better already. I slide my money across the counter, tip my hat, and leave.

I'm on the last stretch, and the streets are now swarming with teenagers. They're probably no happier to be back at school than the teachers, but they do a good job of hiding it. The young ones are barely in their teens, just out of *scuola media*, whereas the older ones—chatting, smoking, and flirting—now seem like proper young people, soon to be off to university.

"*Ciao*, Prof!"

"*Ciao*, Philip!"

"Good Morning, Mr. Jones!"

I smile and give a brief wave to them all and a "*Ciao*" or a "Good morning" depending on whether I remember that I should be speaking to them in English. I think back to the LED display outside the *farmacia* and try to shake the remaining dark thoughts from my head. Venice will be okay, I think to myself. Because one day this lot—bright, funny, creative, and frequently a little bit noisier than I'd like—will be in charge of it. As long as they stay. That's the crux of it. As long as they stay. Over the years, I realize, I have taught something like two percent of the population of the city. You might think that I'd constantly be running into ex-students. Not so. Locals are so often invisible, submerged in the crowds of visitors. Anonymous Venetians.

"So why did you come to Venice?" Someone asks me this in every class. Which means that, by a conservative estimate, I've been asked it well over one hundred times by now.

"Because it was the city that my wife and I loved most in all the world." The answer, banal as it might seem, is an honest one and rarely changes. But sometimes I'll add a little more: Because we wanted to live somewhere where everything was so beautiful.

And I realize now, that that was not enough in itself. Or, more precisely, that if the physical beauty of the city was what drew us in, it would not have been enough to keep us here. Don't get me wrong: My wife Caroline and I still joke that there are no problems so serious that they can't be solved by a spritz outside Nico's, looking out onto the Giudecca Canal. Or simply by sitting outside on the *vaporetto* journey to work, trying to ignore the freezing cold and thinking what an extraordinary thing it is to be travelling to work by boat, and how lucky, oh how very lucky, I am to be able to see the sun rising over the Grand Canal as part of my daily commute.

That isn't enough. Not on its own. The truth is that all that beauty, all that truly awe-inspiring beauty, is not enough. It will not, by itself, make you happy. So why did we stay? Simply because we settled down, as we always have, found work and met nice people? No, that would also be too easy an answer. Perhaps the best I can come up with is that the experience of living in this city has changed us, in the way that no other city has. Despite the petty irritations of day-to-day living, despite the fears over its future, this city somehow continues to work. It continues, against extraordinary odds, to survive. The newspapers may be full of headlines about corruption, mismanagement, a declining population, and unmanageable hordes of tourists; but there is something about it that contrives to knock the cynicism out of you. There is, quite simply, still a magic to it, and that magic can change you. It may be that, one day, the city will no longer cast the same spell over us as once it did; and then, perhaps, it will be time to move on. I hope that day never comes. I hope that living here never becomes quite normal.

Will we ever feel like Venetians? I don't think so. I think we came here too late in life for that. There will always be something a little bit "foreign" about us. That's okay. And for much of the time—whether it be trying to explain to a class why *Santo Stefano* is called

Boxing Day in English, or wishing a work colleague "Happy Birthday" in Welsh—that "otherness" isn't such a bad thing.

You really have to want to live in this city. This city that needs to be loved a little more, and taken a little less for granted. Six years on from that day when a water taxi deposited us at Campo San Barnaba, with ten pieces of luggage and nothing so much as a permanent address—we still do.

Biography

Philip Gwynne Jones was born in South Wales in 1966 and lived and worked throughout Europe before settling in Scotland in the 1990s. He first came to Italy in 1994, when he spent some time working for the European Space Agency in Frascati, a job that proved to be less exciting than he had imagined. Philip now works as a teacher, writer, and translator, and lives in Venice with Caroline. He is the author of the crime novels The Venetian Game *and* Vengeance in Venice *(both published by Constable) and the travel memoir* The Venice Project. *For those who wish to practice their Italian,* The Venetian Game *is also available in translation as* Il Ponte dei Delitti.

Further information can be found at
philipgwynnejones.com
Facebook @philipgwynnejones
Twitter @PGJonesVenice

"Paradise Garden—Where I Can Find the Real Venice" by Iris Loredana

In Venice, each garden and plant could tell a story, and the garden I grew up in is no exception. It's an ancient, inspiring, and energizing garden that taught me, above all, that there are *two Venices*. And it tells me that the ancient Venice still exists. Take a look *beyond* the familiar façades of our town and you'll discover that there's a whole *private* city behind the scenes, consisting of *horti conclusi,* forgotten courtyard gardens. They hide behind red brick walls and are never visible to passersby. It's an unknown city where the true vocation and origin of Venice have survived, after all. This unknown city is rather large because private gardens make up almost half the surface of Venice.

Exploring the hidden, private Venice has been my favorite pastime since I was a child. During the long school summer holidays, I used to slip away from the house on hot afternoons and spend hours on end in the cool and leafy courtyard of the Greek Orthodox Church, San Giorgio dei Greci, reading or chatting with friends. Sometimes, I sat on a white marble bench under an olive tree, recalling the stories my father had told me the evening before. He used to tell all kinds of stories, of Venice and Constantinople, spices and Levantine gardens built around exotic and forgotten recipes.

As a child, you get the opportunity to bond with the city even deeper, and I did make use of this privilege, exploring every nook and cranny of my neighborhood, which is San Zaccaria and San Giorgio dei Greci. By the time I was ten years old, I had made up my mind that I was going to explore and write about this second, private Venice, the city I couldn't recognize in guides or art books for tourists. Venice, this lively, kind and humane city, the last remaining *polis* of the world as one of my best friends calls her, still exists. Yet, most visitors just don't know where to start to look for it. In the maze of *calli* and *campielli*, one can get lost so easily but then, there's a red thread to follow, but you must be prepared that it will lead you in a surprising direction.

In my opinion, if you really wish to explore Venice, the first tool you need is a *map in your mind* consisting of stories opening the doors to this secret, forgotten world, where the authentic Venice has survived. Venice today is so crowded, but her core is still here, untouched and hiding from prying eyes.

Especially my neighborhood, the part of Venice I know best, could tell a few memorable stories. The one I'm telling you here is how you can step back in time in a special garden. It was created in the fourth century AD, which makes it the oldest garden in Venice, and for a few centuries, it was also the largest in town. All you need to do is enter a little red house overlooking a narrow *campiello*, walk up a white marble staircase, and there it is, lush and green and filled with flowers, just like it must have looked hundreds of years ago.

But first, you must cross a bridge. It's called *Ponte della Canonica,* the oldest stone bridge in town built in the year 1170. Even at 6:00 a.m., sleepy tourists are stopping here, taking pictures of the Bridge of Sighs just ahead, shimmering in a rose-tangerine hue, while the only sound you can hear are martins circling above the city in the balmy morning sun.

Without noticing, you just stepped on historical territory, yet, this isn't clear, for the *campo* (Venetian square) beyond the bridge looks like an average Venetian *al fresco* living room, enveloped in a smell of fresh brioche coming from a bakery and *bacari*-style restaurants, wine bars, and the rustic corner coffee shop.

Here, you stop for a minute and watch the barmen arrange *tramezzini* and chocolate-cream filled croissants. This is the type of croissant you will only find in Venice, buttery, warm, soft and crispy at the same time. Yet, you turn towards the archway in front of you, behind which a glowing white and polished church façade demands attention. While quickly crossing a narrow *campo*, you don't notice that little house painted in *rosso veneziano*—Venetian red, whose windowsills are adorned with geranium and rosemary pots. Only for a second do you stop to try to find out where that scented cloud of heavy vanilla and zesty lemon balm has come from. But then, you might as well forget about that beckoning scent and continue walking onto more familiar territory, the *vaporetto* world of Riva degli Schiavoni.

You just walked past my neighborhood AND the oldest garden in town. The flowery scent came from this garden, forgotten while it hides behind the buildings you just passed by on your left. In 400 AD, it was called *El Brolo*, a rambling vineyard-orchard spreading across two islands whose names sound strange as well, for who recalls *Ombriola* and *Le Gemine?* These names make up the authentic, *second* Venice, whose map may sound completely unfamiliar to tourists in our times.

El Brolo, the garden, once belonged to the nuns of the first monastery built in Venice, San Zaccaria. In 826 AD, the nuns donated a large portion of their garden to the fledgling Republic to build a Doge's Palace and a chapel, later called *Basilica di San Marco*. The garden soon changed its name and became known as *Piazza San Marco*—St. Mark's Square.

El Brolo stretched all along the Grand Canal to where San Moisè is located today, at a time when Venice still was called *Le Venetie*, a loose agglomerate of reed-covered islands. San Zaccaria was founded at the same time as Santa Fosca in Torcello was, and soon, it became a lively place populated with merchants from Constantinople, Greece, Egypt, Syria, and Dalmatia, whose boats were moored along Riva degli Schiavoni. The nuns didn't like the noise and crowds, so they had a wall built to protect their garden, and a wooden door was closed at night. Only one public entrance remained, the church and guest house opening up on Campo San Provolo. The former guest house is the little red building I mentioned above. German nuns lived here until 1968, when Grandmother Lina, who writes the blog *La Venessiana* with me, and her family bought the red house and its terraced gardens. In less than ten years, they created a verdant paradise, and I think that's what the monastery gardens of San Zaccaria must have looked like for centuries. This garden became my favorite place on earth and its story the main inspiration for writing a blog whose purpose is to show readers that there is a second Venice, the ancient city that has survived, though often not accessible to visitors.

When I was a child, in the 1980s and 1990s, Grandfather took care of the gardenscape. He told me a thousand stories about gardening in the Lagoon, its rewards, challenges, and particularities. Even though she just turned 95, Grandmother Lina still takes care of the plants. A few years ago, she returned home with pink carnations from San Francesco della Vigna. She was given a rose bush from

San Lazzaro degli Armeni twenty years ago, and there are other plants on the terrace that could tell a story.

In May 1992, I sat on the terrace one day while Grandfather was watering the plants and made a drawing, complete with description of all the herbs, flowers, trees, and shrubs. There were tall plants growing in terracotta pots, one yucca, two aralias, a few palm trees, and soft green ferns. A pergola was overgrown with *uva fragola* grapes. Purple wisteria and climbing pink roses were thriving next to white and red blossoming oleander. I was enchanted by the scent of fragrant jasmine and pittosporum, blossoming next to each other. In the garden below, the level where salt water puddles sometimes form during high tides, blue lilies and a red maple tree were growing, just like today, next to an old cedar, pomegranate trees, kitchen laurel, strawberries, red currents, and pink hydrangea. The air was filled with the scent of lily of the valley, blossoming in pots arranged in a protected corner of the terrace. And there was a geranium plant whose petals Grandmother used to make syrup.

Today, the garden has changed, like all gardens do, and the first impression you get now is a fluffy cloud of white, pink, and red blossoms. It was—and still is—such a quiet garden. When you live in Venice, you can hear the sounds of footsteps at all times of the day. This garden is different, and it seems that our jungle somehow muffles every noise except the chirping voices of the birds.

The kitchen garden is still there and Grandmother's four staple herbs that she considers essential for cooking in the Venetian manner. She's got parsley, chocolate-flavored mint, Moroccan mint, lemon-flavored sage, and spike lavender. Herbs from the Dolomiti mountains flourish here, sweet woodruff and chives, doing surprisingly well in a quiet corner in the shade. There's *erba cristallina*, anise mint and rosemary, tomatoes, eggplants, courgettes, and a variety of *lattughe*, soft salads of the Lagoon.

This is a *giardino movimentato*, stretching across several levels, which means that a greater variety of plants can be grown, so important in Venice. I think that Lina succeeded in turning back time and prolonging the life of the ancient monastery garden. This is just one example how the original Venice is still there, just a few steps from where the crowds are passing. There is this second city after all, surviving in an unexpected way, lovingly tended by the Venetians.

Biography

Iris Loredana, CSR / Sustainability / Slow Food expert and author of La Venessiana - The Fragrant World of Venice. La Venessiana *is a slow travel, garden, and food guide, founded by Iris and her Grandmother Lina in June 2015. They show visitors the hidden Venice, never told in guidebooks, her forgotten stories, gardens, and recipes.*

Visit lavenessiana.com

"Venice in the Mind" by Barbara Lynn-Davis

I bet I'm the only person contributing to this book who hasn't been to Venice in almost twenty years. The last time I went, as leader of a tour group for a grad school friend who hurt her back and found herself suddenly unable to go, I had no sense it would be my last. But looking back, it seems obvious. I stayed in a comfortable tourist hotel near San Marco, I remember virtually nothing of the trip except one dim image of being in the Church of San Zaccaria, in front of the Bellini altarpiece, and I spent a lot of time holding a silver-framed picture of my then-one-year-old daughter, missing her horribly and wanting to go home. Yup, the spell was gone.

My daughter was one excuse for not returning in the years after this trip: I wasn't inspired to go back with her and risk spending our time chasing pigeons. And then, money was tight and a trip to Italy or anywhere across the ocean was, to be frank, out of the question. The most exotic trip we took in these years as a young family was to Quebec—and that was to get our dog. Venice seemed like a distant, enchanted other life I had once lived, especially the year in the mid-1990s researching my dissertation on pastoral landscape—mornings in the Marciana Library in the company of some old tome, a quick *traghetto* ride across the canal to make it to the shops before they closed for *pranzo*, afternoon naps with my husband, jasmine-scented nights. Now, our lives were all about making a home in New England.

It's in these "practical" New England years though—I'd left academics by this time and started selling real estate—that Venice burrowed deeply into my mind. I'd gotten the idea for a historical novel set in Venice, what later became *Casanova's Secret Wife*. I researched the book, sure. I read lots of books, miraculously delivered to my doorstep by then-new Amazon. And I painted my study a soft rose smudged with a sponge to remind me of faded Venetian rococo walls. But I never went back to Venice, and I never even thought about going back. I wrote the whole book from my head, recalling palaces, hidden courtyards, and pocket gardens where I used to love to lean in, drinking in the perfumes escaping from rusted iron gates. I stepped in and out of shiny black gondolas conjured for myself, took imagined trips out to islands in the lagoon.

Crossed bridges into the Jewish *Ghetto*. Relived sexy afternoons in bed.

Venice in the mind.

I was sure when I finished writing the book (which took me ten years—as these "practical" years were filled with other responsibilities), I would triumphantly return to Venice. Maybe I would launch the book there, throw a big party and serve Bellinis and dress up eighteenth-century style. I would walk the streets again, revisit spots that I had included in the book. I would poke around the convent of Santa Maria degli Angeli, where the nuns in my story lived, disused now but where architectural remnants survive. *I would ... I would ...* but now, a year after the book has been published and with no plans in sight, I am starting to recognize that something holds me from going back.

There's the usual, "It could never be what it once was to me." And that's partly true. I had first discovered Venice in the 1980s, as an intern at the Peggy Guggenheim Collection. I'd moved out of the group intern house where I'd started my time there, as I had been given the worst room, the one right off the kitchen. It was noisy, and I was sleepless and miserable. It was also full of mosquitoes. I moved in with an 86-year-old Yugoslavian *contessa* in her apartment along the Zattere. She was one tough cookie, earning income by renting out the best room in the house, the one overlooking the Giudecca Canal, and also cooking for a friend who came over each day for *pranzo*. (This relationship fascinated me, the old *contessa* cooking a traditional meal for the unmarried professional woman, filling the midday Italian hours, which are only pleasurable if you have a family at home.)

In any event, this stay in Venice was curative and even a bit magical for me. I had most recently been living in New York City, working at the Guggenheim Museum there. What had started as a love affair with THAT city had turned into a get-me-out-of-here: I'd lost my amazing sublet in Greenwich Village and ended up in Hoboken, New Jersey, an hour's commute from work; one particularly unappetizing day, a fat, gristly rat had jumped across my path as I walked around the reservoir near the museum. Poor, frazzled, and hating modern life in general, the chance to leave it all behind and go to Venice filled a yearning within me. In Venice, I used to sit along the Zattere on sunny afternoons and stare out to the looming machinery of the industrial mainland just a few miles away, happy to be away from all the ugliness, the smells and pollution, yet at the same time, seeing it threatening there on the horizon. I wished it would all be gone.

That's what Venice came to be for me: *the dream that it would all be gone.* A full immersion into the past, where everything truly looked as it once did: the whole city, not just a little *centro storico* you eventually find nestled within the sprawl. So I think this is really why I don't go back: the Internet (sigh, more of modern life, spreading its tentacles everywhere and invading my dreamscape) has brought me pictures of cruise ships disgorging thousands into the city each day; stories of 20 million tourists a year, trash left behind by hoards of careless day trippers, the question posed, *Should the city be selling tickets just to enter?*

The truth is, I'm afraid to go back. Of course, Venice was already a touristy place when I lived there. (And it's fashionable to say it's been a touristy place since the eighteenth century, when it was a favorite stop on the Grand Tour. But I think that is an over-simplification.) In any event, there was already talk about Venice being a "dying" city, with few restaurants serving authentic cuisine and neighborhoods taken over by cheap glass and mask shops. But you could avoid all this in little corners of experience: you could make your own Venice within Venice. Just as Piazza San Marco hardly appears in my book, so it was not the heart of my own life in Venice. My heart was in Dorsoduro, a couple of blocks from the museum, in silent, slightly rundown courtyards anchored by well heads and filled with cats.

I think this is why the spell of Venice broke for good in that hotel on top of San Marco almost twenty years ago: it was just too much real life for me, in every way: the real need to take a job as a tour guide (quite ill-suited to my personality), the real fact that I missed my daughter more than I craved any art or travel experience. The real infiltration of the city by crowds and pollution and over-commoditization. Venice has become too real for me, and as such, only has a place in my mind.

Biography

After graduating from Brown University with a degree in art history, Barbara Lynn-Davis worked at the Peggy Guggenheim Museum in Venice and began a life-long love affair with the lagoon city. She returned to Venice for a year while completing her Ph.D. in Renaissance art at Princeton University. Along the way, she discovered the memoirs of famed lover Giacomo Casanova and found the story she wanted to tell: Casanova's Secret Wife *(Kensington Publishing, 2017). Lynn-Davis teaches art history and writing at Wellesley College and lives outside Boston with her family. To learn more, visit barbaralynndavis.com.*

"A Vocal Dead Venetian" by Candace Magner

I talk to dead people. Mostly composers and poets, which makes sense because I am a lyric singer, and much of my career has involved interpreting what was intended by the artists of days gone by. I channel the emotions the songs convey, I get behind the spirit of the epoch, and I sometimes see in my mind's movie theater the actual historic people in their daily lives. I don't mean this in a metaphoric way; it is a superpower, like having eidetic memory or really good eyesight.

So you can imagine the cacophony of ghostly historic voices one might hear in a deeply artistic city like Venice, little changed over the centuries. The *palazzi* ring with the voices (some now disembodied) of singers, actors, orators, writers, politicians, and *pescatori*. The stones of Venice hold the sounds of the footsteps of noblemen visiting the gambling rooms or their paramours.

Before my first visit, I didn't know these sounds. Since there is no other city like Venice where past and present overlap like almost-identical photographs, I had no expectation or judgment of what the experience would be. I was just intending to get away from the turmoil of wedding preparations at my friends' home in Trento.

There are several ways to get to Venice from Trento, and it was becoming clear that none of them was going to be traveled by my friends as the celebrations neared. So I boarded the Valsugana train and enjoyed the breathtaking views through the mountains and down to the plains of the Veneto. I had no pictures in my head of what I was going to see, no guidebooks or maps or movies or photos. But I had heard the call of the voices of the poets and musicians, and suddenly here I was.

Outside the Santa Lucia station, I viewed Venice as a virgin and heard my own voice say, "Thank goodness. I'm back." Which was odd, because I thought I was the only one inside my head, and I knew I hadn't been here in this lifetime.

My second thought was, "I need a project here."

My project was immediately clear: a deeper look into the life and works of the most published composer of the seventeenth century. Not Monteverdi (who was already talking to me) or Cavalli, whose operas had already thrilled me, but a woman named Barbara

Strozzi, whose songs and cantatas I would come to know intimately. Thus started the decades-long work that leads me to Venice again and again.

Barbara started pulling me all over the city—to Santa Sofia, her natal parish; to Santi Apostoli where she raised her children. To the *Archivio di Stato* and the *Biblioteca Marciana* where I learned how to find and read the documents that related to her life. To the parish archives housed at Sant'Apollonia, to the Church of Santa Maria e San Donato in Murano, to a guy who knew about a church that had been gone for 200 years, to the *campi* and *calli* that now hold only the names of the earliest opera theatres in the world.

She even led me, one rainy evening, to her own house, where thanks to some kind workmen fixing the entryway, I was able to see inside to the original staircase that had been covered up for centuries by some prior reconstruction.

My research turned up lots of tidbits about Barbara's life. Most of her music publications were housed in libraries outside Venice, taking me to Florence and Bologna to continue my collecting. One work was known to have completely disappeared. And one piece was, tantalizingly, kept in Venice—and part of it was known to be missing.

Now, before you think I'm just imagining things, I have to reveal my other superpower (and I do only have two of them). I can find lost objects. I've always been able to do this: my dad's retriever dogs would steal some object and hide it for safekeeping. I would close my eyes and see where it was, and off we'd go to fetch it. Or my spouse would drive off to work and return ten minutes later: "I forgot my badge. And now I can't find it on my desk." "Did you look in the refrigerator? Check the vegetable crisper drawer." And there it would be.

To the Correr collection I went, only to find that the manuscript I wanted was loaned to the library at *Conservatorio di Musica Benedetto Marcello*. Which was rarely open. The consultation hours were limited, and I was running out of time during the research trip. I wanted to have a microfilm of the extant music, just to enjoy what might have been if the manuscript were complete.

At last in the conservatory library, sitting alone at the big table, I scanned through the book until I found the music with Barbara's name on it. It was a long and complex piece, and yes, it ended abruptly and a new piece started. Barbara, oh Barbara, where can it be, this missing end of your song?

Because I have superpowers, I could hear the voice of the composer, now "my" composer, telling me to keep leafing through the manuscript. And because I can find lost objects, I recognized the missing pages that had been rearranged when the book was repaired some time in the distant past.

Because on that first visit I knew that I had returned to Venice, I keep listening to Barbara's voice. She showed me other manuscripts in unexpected towns in Europe. She led me to the historic workshop of an instrument maker and to the documents that suggest she might well have owned one of his delicate small guitars (a copy of which I now play to accompany her songs). She introduced me to current members of the *Compagnia de Calza "I Antichi"* who continue the traditions of the libertine philosophers of the sixteenth and seventeenth centuries and who invited me to join their celebrations as the incarnation of La Strozzi.

The disembodied voices of the 1600s urged me to be brave, to speak Italian to everyone, to ask crazy questions, to learn some Venetian, to decipher old handwriting, to peruse antique legal documents, to learn the traditions and the history. They led me down dark *calli* in the dead of night to learn the timeless music of water on marble and footsteps on *masegni*, to walk the twists and turns in the neighborhoods and get lost, to recognize the skyline, to explore the Lido of Malamocco where the merchant ships would await cargo for export.

Strozzi's whisperings introduced me to the chapel choir of San Marco, let me sing from the organ loft in that great basilica, and to make rowdy music during Carnevale. She encouraged me to come spend the summer playing opera written by her teacher Cavalli.

Even after more than twenty years, I ask her daily to show me hidden treasures from her life so I can share them with the world. I've now published 120 of her musical works and encouraged performers on six continents to spread her vocal music. She is persistent, bossy even.

That which is still lost, I hope she will tell me where to find. And that she will continue to lure me back to Venice for the very first time.

Biography

Candace Magner is a musicologist, singer, and baroque guitarist living in New Mexico. Her studies in baroque continuo began when she located a missing manuscript of Barbara Strozzi and began to edit it. Her comprehensive website on Strozzi is frequently cited by researchers: BarbaraStrozzi.com.

She is general editor and publisher at Cor Donato Editions, CorDonatoEditions.com, which publishes Barbara Strozzi: The Complete Works. *Her scholarly editions are used around the world.*

"Never Leaving, Always Returning"
by Luca Marchiori

The hotel receptionist brought up the reservation on the computer screen. "Oh!" she said, her face lighting up as if she had just won the lottery. "You've got a Venetian name!"

"Yes," I replied, "I was born here."

"Well, sir, welcome home!"

This scene has played many times in my life since, back in the 1970s, my family formed part of the mass exodus that started the depopulation of Venice. First, many moved to the mainland suburb of Mestre, attracted by cheaper housing and shop prices, the convenience of having a car, yet being able to kid themselves that they'd not really left since they were still living within the boundaries of the *Comune di Venezia*. Then my uncle was the first to leave the *comune* completely, moving to Piemonte, where his wife was from. Then it was our turn. My mother being English, we went much further afield and ended up living in her hometown of Bournemouth, a seaside resort on the south coast of England.

But you don't just leave Venice, at least not if that's where you're from, and my roots there go back a long way. At the time of the republic, my family were *cittadini originari*, part of the middle class of merchants, lawyers, civil servants, who steered the ship of state under the direction of their political masters, the *nobili*. The name "Marchiori" runs throughout the records of the *Archivio di Stato* like letters stamped through a piece of seaside rock. It's literally carved in stone on the front of the Chiesa di San Rocco where several statues were added in the eighteenth century by a certain Giovanni Marchiori.

I don't remember a time in my life when Venice didn't exist for me. Some of my earliest memories, backed up by hefty photograph albums, are of being mugged of bird seed by pigeons in the Piazza San Marco, or of riding one of the *leoncini*, the red marble lion statues to the side of the Basilica. For me, my love of Venice is that of a child for its mother, a matter in which you have no choice, which has immense rewards, but also responsibilities.

Like many emigrants, who are also immigrants somewhere, I have spent my life being treated as "other" in both my host and original cultures. However, my father, who never quite got over leaving Italy, instilled an innate sense of "Venetianness" in me. Comfort foods of my childhood included *risi e bisi*, a pea risotto that the Doge used to eat on the feast of San Marco, and the days of the week in Venetian dialect rolled off my tongue as easily as the English versions. He made us live his own version of the Venetian maxim *"prima veneziani e poi cristiani"* (first Venetian and then Christian): *"prima veneziani e poi inglesi."*

At first, we travelled back to Italy every summer, but the endless round of visits to friends and family, coupled with the two-thousand-mile round trip with two young children in the back of a Ford Escort, began to make my parents wish for holidays that were a bit more of a break. And so, it was that at the age of nine or ten, my first year passed in which I didn't set foot in the Piazza but instead paddled on a Spanish beach.

Within a year or so, however, my older brother and I were deemed old enough to travel on our own, and we were sent to Piemonte to spend the summer with my uncle and his family, at the end of which my father came to meet us and to take us for a few days to Venice. For my brother, one or two summers were enough, but I continued this arrangement alone for the rest of my teenage years.

When my grandfather died, instead of visiting Piemonte, I would go and stay with his widow, my step-grandmother, who lived near the train station in Mestre. Every morning, armed with Giulio Lorenzetti's *Venice and its Lagoon* and a teenage plan to visit every *calle, campo*, and *chiesa* in the city, I would set off across the Ponte della Libertà, achieving this aim within three years, and much more besides. Many of the facts and figures my teenage brain assimilated at this time were later to form the basis of my blog, *Luca's Venice*.

It was at this time that I reconnected with many of my Venetian family, including my cousin who had just qualified as an architect after years studying at the University of Venice Ca' Foscari, and my musical cousins and aunt, who lived, appropriately, a stone's throw from La Fenice. When, finally, time came for me to go to university, I made my choice of Manchester, based on the presence of one

Professor Brian Pullan, through whom I was able to begin serious study of the history of the Venetian Republic.

It wasn't until much later in my life—after a period of about ten years in which I forsook the city completely—that I finally had the opportunity to spend a much larger part of my time in the city. Of course, Venice today is not the Venice I remember as a child and teenager but is rather the Venice of mass tourism and the *navi grandi*, where the families of glass animals in the shops are more likely to be made in China than in Murano, and the scent of fast food restaurants mingles with that of incense in the Church of San Zuan Grisostomo.

Interestingly, in the 1980s there was a home-grown fast food restaurant in Campo San Luca called Italy & Italy, which served beer and wine as well as fizzy drinks. This is long gone, the site occupied by a clothes shop, and Venetian hamburgers are supplied by chains with Scottish or regal names.

But a lot of the old Venice still exists exactly how I remember it. In *A Room with a View,* E.M. Forster has his character Eleanor Lavish note how every city has its own distinctive smell, and indeed Venice has many. For me, however, the most distinctive smell of Venice is one of damp bricks and mortar drying out in warm summer air, rather like the scent of a wine cellar. You come across it by chance, in the city's narrow back alleys, and it always takes me back to the days when the fifteen-year-old Luca sat eating gelato on the bench in Campo de Santa Maria Nova, marveling at the sight of the Chiesa dei Miracoli even though he'd seen it a million times before.

This smell fills my mind with ghostly memories of Venice past that seem to coexist superimposed over Venice present. For me, it's as if the old beggar, who used to wish passersby a *"buon giorno"* on the Ponte dei Zogatoli, has just popped around the corner, or that I could still go and use the international pay phones to call my mother from the central post office in the Fontego dei Tedeschi, now a luxury department store.

I can still go and enjoy a *mozzarella in carrozza* from the Rosticceria Gislon, which hasn't changed at all since my father first took me there as his father had done before. It's getting harder and harder to fight your way past the queues for the new *gelateria* next door, but it's one of a few places in Venice that hasn't changed one bit in 40 or more years.

That my life has constantly taken me away from Venice seems to me a most Venetian thing. My ancestors, the merchants of Venice, would have spent much of their time overseas on the trade routes, and on returning, I get to share their experience of excitement as they arrived back in the city after what could have been years away. For if Venice is in your blood, you always will return and even when you are away, you can never really escape, for like your mother, you are part of her and so where you are, she is.

Biography

Luca Marchiori is a writer, editor, teacher, and blogger. Born in Venice but raised in Bournemouth in the United Kingdom, he has also lived in Switzerland and France as well as the UK and his native Italy. He currently divides his time between Venice, Rome, Tuscany, and the UK where he writes about his twin passions of Venice and Italian food. Luca's writing has been published in various magazines such as Great Italian Chefs, *the* Independent, *and* Tuscanyicous, *the official website of the Tuscan Tourist Board. He is soon to be seen talking about Venice in an episode of Netflix's* Somebody Feed Phil. *Read more at lucasitaly.com.*

"Venetian Baptism" by Greg Mohr

There are two kinds of gondoliers: those who *have* fallen in the water, and those who are *going to* fall in the water. I have personally been "unexpectedly baptized" three times so far.

Perhaps I'm getting ahead of myself here.

As I write this, I'm planning a trip to Venice.

There are very few things I love more than writing about Venice and her boats, but one of those things is going there.

I was born Gregory Edward Mohr, and while my driver's license and passport identify me as such, many people know me as "Gondola Greg." I am, without question, the most ridiculously obsessed human being in the English-speaking world when it comes to gondolas.

I proposed to my wife on one and have been operating them in Newport Beach, California, since 1993. We've operated gondolas in Texas, Nevada, and a few other US cities. So far, I haven't had the opportunity to actually live in Venice, although it's on my bucket list. Instead, my family and I have made several pilgrimages to the city that means so much to us—usually staying for a week or more in a rented apartment.

I've spent nearly half my life now on gondolas, and I truly feel like a man who's found his "calling." There is nothing I'd rather do. You know you're obsessed when you find yourself at 30,000 feet, looking down from an airplane window, you see some random lake, river, canal, or ocean inlet, and you think, "Hey, I'd like to row a gondola there."

Early on in my fanaticism, I made contact with a guy in Padova who'd grown up in Venice. The Internet was young, and he was involved with web design and photography. The man's name was Nereo Zane. We corresponded for a while, and when I arrived in Venice for the first time, Nereo brought me to a rowing club where an old friend of his was coaching.

This was a real life dream come true. I spent every day for a week, out on the water, with Maestro Arturo Moruccio coaching and Nereo translating. The club is the Gruppo Sportivo Voga Veneta in Mestre. Often referred to as the GSVVM, the club is on the mainland, across from Venice, right where the long bridge to Venice begins to cross the water.

Arturo was in his seventies and in better shape than I was in my thirties. He had the hoarse voice of a swim coach, and he only spoke one word in English: "STOP!" (which he used a lot as our training sessions progressed). We rowed several different types of Venetian boats. I learned how to navigate from both front and back positions in a tandem boat. I joined three other club members to row a four-man *sandolo*. Arturo even taught me the strange scissor-like style of rowing known as "*valesana*"—where you use two oars that are crossed.

On my first day of training, I found humility in an unexpected way.

I'd spent a lot of time preparing for this, had received training from a very competent American gondolier, and expected to at least *look* like I knew what I was doing on the back of a boat. We took out a gondola from the club's fleet. It looked just like the one I had back in California, except that it was bright orange and blue (the colors of the rowing club). Once we got out on the water and Arturo handed me the oar, I stepped up onto the back of the boat, and something was definitely wrong. The boat was remarkably tippy. I could hardly keep my balance. Every single wave or boat wake sent the gondola wallowing back and forth, and each time one of us shifted our weight, the boat reacted more than I was accustomed to. Embarrassed about looking so incompetent, I asked my friend Nereo if there was something different about the boat. He and Arturo exchanged a few sentences in Venetian dialect, and then he explained to me that it was a "racing gondola"—which meant that while the boat had the same dimensions as a passenger gondola, it was much lighter. I had one of those "throw out everything you thought you knew" kind of moments.

As we trained, Arturo put me in more and more challenging situations. We rowed in an area where cargo barges travel. In the mornings they chug slowly towards the island city loaded with goods, but in the afternoons they're empty. The captains always seem to be in a hurry to get back. I often found myself navigating those waters in the afternoons, as barge captains plowed by, leaving huge rolling waves through which I needed to survive. I always managed to keep my footing, albeit sometimes just barely. Honestly,

I hated it at the time, but now I realize how much the experience helped me.

I learned to become one with the boat—to feel the water through the boat. To do so, I was rowing barefoot to make for a much clearer connection. (I also learned the consequences of not putting sunscreen on the tops of my feet).

At the end of each day there was fellowship, reflection, and talk of what we would cover the next day as we gathered at the club. Drinks and food were local, and they were unbelievably good. When Venetians "throw something together" and serve it with wine that was made "just up the road," you never want to leave.

One hot afternoon, I was out rowing with my friend Nereo and Maestro Arturo. Because Arturo spoke zero English, and at the time my grasp of Italian was equally nonexistent, there was a lot of pantomime—as well as translation by my patient friend Nereo.

We entered the city through the Cannaregio Canal, passed under the Tre Archi Bridge, turned down the Grand Canal, and stopped just short of the Rialto Bridge. We tied the gondola up next to the fish market, and Arturo showed us a little cave of a wine bar. We stepped down into a basement-like room, where wine was kept in huge wicker-wrapped bottles on the cold stone floor. It was the "house red," poured from a plastic siphon tube into my glass. I hadn't expected to be given red wine on a hot day … and I certainly hadn't expected it to be so refreshing. I credit the cold stone floor for naturally chilling it.

As we stood there sipping chilled red, elbows against the bar, Arturo decided that "the kid" (that would be me) needed to try a sort of delicacy. He said something in Venetian dialect to the girl behind the bar, and she produced for us … three whole cuttlefish. Arturo laughed, and in his swim-coach voice gave what sounded like instructions. Barking what I can only imagine was, "Look here, you Hollywood poser: *this* is how it's done!" he popped the tiny squid in his mouth and away it went. Smiling, Nereo followed with the same ritual (minus the apparent insults).

And then it was my turn. I thought to myself, this looks a bit like the old fraternity goldfish-swallowing hazing ritual. I took a slug of cool *rosso* from my glass, tipped my head back, and down the hatch went the cuttlefish! I could be imagining it, but I think I won Arturo over a little bit at that point. We rowed for the rest of the day, and I came away with expert coaching … and another great story.

On the last day of rowing instruction, we took that orange and blue gondola out one more time. Arturo and I rowed the boat as a tandem team, while my wife and our youngest daughter rode as passengers.

We rowed that gorgeous boat down the Grand Canal on a sunny September afternoon. At one point a *vaporetto* rumbled by with about thirty Japanese tourists snapping photos of us. I imagined them going home and showing their families the "real Venetian gondoliers" they saw on their trip.

We rowed back across the lagoon to the club as the sun was approaching the horizon.

When you take a club boat out, you lower it into the water; afterwards, you hoist it up and bring it back to where the fleet of vessels is stored. It had been a gorgeous day, and a lot of club members were by the hoist as Arturo and I arrived. Dozens of club members and friends stood along the large concrete *fondamenta*, watching as the boats lined up between the submerged hoisting straps and were then lifted out of the water.

As I rowed our gondola towards the hoist, I felt great—like I'd truly "arrived." I'd spent a week trying to prove to everyone in the GSVVM club that I wasn't just some "California wanna-be." I'd put in a lot of work, and it seemed like everyone was finally taking me seriously.

Arturo was in the front of the boat, and I had been entrusted with the rowing position on the back of the boat. This is known as *"pope"* (or po-pay, as it is pronounced)—it means that you're the captain of the boat. With everyone watching, Arturo and I maneuvered the vessel in between the straps. Once it was in position, we needed to keep the gondola in place until the hoist operator raised those straps up to lift it out of the water. Everything seemed fine, and then, I noticed that the back of the gondola was drifting towards the concrete *fondamenta*.

Obviously, I didn't want the tail of the boat to grind against that rough surface, especially with everyone watching, so I reached out to place my hand against the wall. It seemed like the right thing to do, but what I didn't realize was that Arturo was about to do a little flip-of-the-wrist trick with his oar; this maneuver quickly spun the boat to prevent that collision.

So there I was, having reached out to push off of a wall that was suddenly about five feet further away than it had been right before I made my move.

The fall was inevitable.

If I'd played it smart, I would have simply let it happen and caught the rail of the boat as I descended. This would have resulted in the lower half of my body getting wet, and it would have allowed me to rescue some of my dignity and crawl back onto the tail of the boat.

But did I do that?

No. I didn't.

Instead, I made a profoundly stupid decision.

I leaped like some kind of human tree frog, flew through the air, and grabbed hold of a *palina* (a wooden pole, very similar to a telephone pole).

Dozens of Venetians gasped as I performed such an unexpected feat of acrobatics.

Remarkably, I managed to get a hold of that *palina* with both hands and both feet. *Bare* feet.

For about two seconds I perched there (again: think tree frog), and then gravity took over. I slid all the way down that wooden pole, slicing up the bottoms of both feet and the palms of my hands.

Again, more gasping from the gallery of spectators.

Once at the bottom of the *palina*, I planted both freshly-cut feet deep in the mud at the bottom of the lagoon.

It was a true "remember me this way" moment.

A painful walk was followed by lots of sterilization and wound dressing. The club members were good sports about it, and we all enjoyed a good laugh as we toasted with local wine.

As I said before, there are two kinds of gondoliers: those who *have* fallen in the water, and those who are *going to* fall in the water. And while most falls are just that—a simple fall—no one can ever say "Gondola Greg" does things simply.

Not all American gondoliers can say that they've been "baptized in Venetian water," and while I don't recommend my own methods, I'll certainly never forget it.

Biography

Gondola Greg has been a working gondolier in Newport Beach, California, since 1993. He is the president of Gondola Adventures, Inc., with locations in Newport Beach, CA, and Irving, TX (gondola.com), as well as the Gondola Company of Newport in Newport Beach (gondolas.com). He is also president of the Gondola Society of America, and past president of the US Gondola Nationals.

Greg has planned and led several gondola expeditions in different US waterways.

A member of the GSVVM rowing club in Mestre, Italy, Greg has received training from expert coaches in the club.

He's hosted the Gondola Blog (GondolaGreg.com) since August of 2007. When he's not rowing a gondola, or training to race one, he's either painting one ... or painting a picture of a perfect moment on the water for his readers on the Gondola Blog.

"Made in Venice: An Adventure in Artisanship"
by Laura Morelli

The first time I visited Venice as a wide-eyed teenager, I knew I was supposed to go home with Murano glass but I had no idea why.

All I knew was that my friend and I were lured to the famous "glass island" of Murano by a fast-talking hawker in the Piazza San Marco. We were whisked onto an overcrowded, stinky boat. Arriving on Murano, we were pressed into a bustling group of international travelers. We strained to see over the shoulders of other visitors as a glassmaker placed a long blowpipe into a red-hot furnace. As if by magic, he transformed a molten blob into a beautiful vase. Afterward, we waited in line behind several dozen American and Japanese tourists to pay an exorbitant price for a small trinket. My purchase—a small green fish—brought an end to the bewildering experience.

It's telling, I think, that a naïve girl raised on a farm in America might already have a notion of Murano glass—and other artistic traditions like carnival masks and gondolas—as synonymous with Venice. Though it was my first visit, I already had an idea that "Made in Italy" meant a spirit of tradition and recognition around the world as a benchmark of quality.

Even after my Murano glass-buying debacle, it was the artistic traditions of the world that continued to compel me to travel, and they inspired me to pursue advanced studies in art history. Over the subsequent years, Venice continued to lure me above all.

If you described Venice to someone who had no prior knowledge of it, they might think you were making it up, that it was a place existing only in a fairy tale. It's mind-boggling to think that the entire built environment of Venice—everything from the humblest coffee shop to the grandest church—stands atop thousands of wooden pilings driven into the mud centuries ago. Venice has been described as "impossible," and I think that's a good way to capture its essence.

Today, when I stroll along the alleys and quaysides, I imagine what Venice must have been like some five hundred years ago: a city-as-artisanal-factory, its doors open to the streets, its wares spilling out onto the cobblestones. It is easy to conjure the ring of the blacksmith's hammer and aroma of hot coals from the forge; to imagine woodworkers, painters, and gilders sweeping sawdust flecked with red pigments out into the alleys from the thresholds of their doors. That's because, in spite of cycles of decline and renewal in its artisanal enterprises over the past centuries, Venice maintains its place as a world capital of the handmade, the beautiful, the richly colored, the impossibly ornate.

Once I began graduate studies, I quickly learned that none of it—not the glass or the masks or leather or pottery or gilding—could be found in my art history textbooks. Instead, I learned about the great Italian artists of the past—Leonardo da Vinci, Michelangelo, and many others. But I knew that there was much more than the names that filled my art history books. The medieval craft guilds may be long gone, but the techniques, the skill, the forms, the knowledge, the *spirit* of Italian tradition is still intact in world-class objects like Murano glass, Florentine leather, maiolica ceramics, even Parmigiano-Reggiano cheese and grappa. These traditions are kept alive in the hands of thousands of Italian artisans who take pride in their regional specialties, so ingrained that even in the twenty-first century the products of their labor are recognized around the world as a mark of quality.

Once I realized the importance of artisanal tradition within Italian culture, I was riveted; I wanted to know everything! It was the beginning of a journey that would take me from the Alps to Palermo and become my obsession for more than a decade. I traveled to Sardinia to watch an 88-year-old woman swiftly work a wooden hand loom her grandmother had taught her to use when she was only five. I journeyed to Umbria to watch a ceramicist paint a rabbit on a terracotta pot, drawing inspiration from a five-hundred-year-old ceramic fragment at his side. I went to the gastronomic capital of Parma to watch an inspector poke an aging ham hock with a horse-bone needle and draw it under his nose to rate its quality compared to thousands of similar specimens he has tested over four decades. And yes, I returned to Venice many times. Eventually, I compiled my work into a guidebook called *Made in Italy*.

Over the course of my fieldwork, it was the *stories* and the people behind these great traditions that captivated me, that kept me moving forward. The contemporary Italian artisans I interviewed, one after another, told me how important it was to them to pass on the torch of tradition to the next generation.

After hearing this story multiple times, I began to wonder what would happen if the successor were not willing or able to take on the duty of carrying that torch of tradition. And as I interviewed the last remaining gondola makers of Venice, the story of *The Gondola Maker*, my first work of fiction, began to take shape. *The Gondola Maker* follows the story of a young man who, as the eldest son, is positioned to inherit his father's gondola-making boat yard. But because of his complicated relationship with his father, not to mention an unexpected family tragedy in the boat yard, he believes that his destiny lies elsewhere. Soon he finds himself drawn to restore an antique gondola with the dream of taking a girl for a ride.

My second novel, *The Painter's Apprentice,* forms a prequel to *The Gondola Maker* and follows the story of a young woman who wants nothing more than to carry on her father's legacy as a master gilder, but finds herself swept up in the drama of the plague outbreak that ravaged Venice in 1510.

As I have returned to Venice over the years—whether to interview artisans, research a novel, or just to enjoy myself or share it with friends—I have watched the flood of international tourists transform the city. Over many trips, I have come to understand that the effects of modern tourism are complex, but that they are not universally bad. The modern tourism industry finds its origins in Venice in the early 1970s, with an initiative that began with the well-intentioned desire to reinvigorate the economy of a crumbling old city. Venetians who remember that era have told me that the city was remarkably quiet back then, full of generations of Venetian families but without the staggering volume of international visitors that the city draws now.

Today, the downsides of tourism are particularly hard-felt: the crushing crowds, controversies surrounding cruise ship traffic, the challenges of water and waste management, and—significantly for me—the problem of cheaply made souvenirs imported from overseas and passed off as authentic. Increasing numbers of carnival masks, glass objects, and other souvenirs flood into Venice, and it's not easy for today's casual visitor to tell the treasures from the trash. Carnival masks, for example, are imported from Asia and passed off as authentic every single day on the streets of Venice. This is true now more than ever before.

Tourism is not all negative, however. The influx of international visitors to Venice means that the appreciation for important historical arts is continually renewed, and there are more resources to support craftspeople. Some Venetian traditions, such as the making of carnival masks, had all but died out until the tourism industry was bolstered in the 1970s. In recent decades, individual makers and family enterprises have planted a flag in the soil to preserve the legacy of the handmade. In the last twenty years, local organizations have sprung up to help sustain and promote artisans who choose these careers, and the Internet has provided many new opportunities.

Still, let's face it: shopping in Venice can be overwhelming. We all want to go home with a special souvenir, but selecting which Murano glass vase or which lace handkerchief to buy can become a bewildering experience. How do you know if you're buying something authentic, something made in Venice, something made in a traditional way? How do you gauge how much you should pay, and how do you know if you're being ripped off? How do you determine if you have fallen prey to one of the city's many tourist traps?

Recently art organizations in Venice have worked to develop trademarks and new alliances to help protect their artistic heritage and to guard against fakes and cheap knockoffs. Legal regulations have also tightened. However, many Venetian artisans tell me that the well-meaning organizations that try to promote traditional artisans are not able to keep up in the face of the overwhelming numbers of visitors. And many visitors do not take the time to understand the historical trades. Instead, they go home with a small trinket made overseas. Either they do not know the difference, or do not care.

Over the last decade, I have personally seen multi-generational artisan shops in Venice close their doors—including paper makers, bookbinders, mask makers, and glass artisans. When I saw my favorite mask-making shop and my favorite paper-maker close their doors forever, I felt as though I had been kicked in the gut. At the same time, I do understand the pressures as well as the tough family decisions that stand behind each closure.

Surely there is some happy medium between accommodating the crowds and preserving the past in this one-of-a-kind city? In terms of authentic shopping, the truth remains that there is no substitute for a knowledgeable buyer. If you know what you are buying, you can put your money where it counts: back into the pockets of Venetian makers and not into those of importers looking to make a quick profit without any connection to Venice at all.

For centuries, Venice has appeared to visitors as a surreal vision, a city rising from the swampy Adriatic lagoon as a complicated jumble of rivulets, exotic palaces, mosaic-encrusted churches, Gothic façades, and candy-striped gondola moorings. A feast for the eyes, Venice takes time to absorb. Even after the years of study, Venice still captivates me like the first time I saw it. I know that I am not alone.

Decades after my first visit to Murano, my little green glass fish still sits on the windowsill of my study as a testament to my love affair with Venice. In choosing to write about the history of Venetian craftsmanship, I hope to have played a small role in preserving Venetian spirit for new visitors who are as wonderstruck as I was, the first time I watched this "impossible" city unfold from the back of a boat.

Biography

Laura Morelli holds a Ph.D. in art history from Yale University, has taught college-level art history in the US and in Italy, and has produced art history lessons for TED-Ed. Laura has contributed pieces about art and authentic travel to National Geographic Traveler, CNN Radio, Italy Magazine, *and* USA TODAY. *Laura is the author of the Authentic Arts guidebook series that includes* Made in Italy *and* Made in Venice. *Her historical novels bring stories from art history to life. Her debut novel,* The Gondola Maker, *won an IPPY, Benjamin Franklin, and a National Indie Excellence Award.*

"The Secrets of Ca' Biondetti" by Jane Mosse

I am sitting at the window of our rented apartment in Dorsoduro watching the traffic on the Grand Canal, a copy of Henry James' *Coxun Fund* in my lap. Directly opposite is the Cassette delle Rose where once Canova, Venice's last great sculptor, had his studio. To its right sits the Ca' Grande, designed by Sansovino who sadly died in 1570 without seeing the house finished as the Corner family were engrossed in arguing over whose share of the family inheritance should be used to pay him.

Every house in Venice has a story to tell but perhaps none more so than this humble abode next to the Guggenheim Museum, a story that has occupied my life for the last nine months.

I first visited Venice in 1975 on one of those lightning tours that tries to take in too much, leaving the traveler exhausted yet hungry for more. One night in the magical city and I couldn't wait to return. Two years later I was back, newly married, for a week of indulgence. My husband was an artist studying the Renaissance at University, so the majority of our time was spent in museums, churches, and galleries viewing masterpieces by Titian and Tintoretto, Veronese and Bellini, until I was gasping for air and longing to just wander the streets. That I did. Alone.

Although Venice is considered to be one of the most romantic cities in the world, it is a joy to wander unaccompanied through the labyrinth of *calli* and canals. Some years later I returned as a single woman. I felt safe in the city, relaxed about walking along dark passageways late at night. I was made welcome in restaurants, and my time at evening class attempting to learn the language paid off, the locals appreciating my efforts to speak their language. I walked for hours, regularly got lost, took hundreds of photos, climbed towers, sat through evening concerts of baroque music, revisited galleries, attended Midnight Mass at St. Mark's at Christmas, welcomed the New Year in in St. Mark's Square, witnessed Carnevale, and had breakfast at Florian's. It was bliss.

I have lost count of how many times I have returned, often alone, drawn back by the magic of the city. I absorbed myself in literature: books written about Venice, novels set against the backdrop of her canvas, diaries and poetry, memoirs and anthologies. It seemed that all the great names had visited this inspirational place and felt the need to respond in writing: Dickens, Hemingway, Goethe, Browning, D.H. Lawrence, Ezra Pound, L.P. Hartley, and, of course, Henry James, the American master of the novel.

I worked hard at learning the language, wanting more than anything to be able to communicate with the Venetians; it was my way of saying, "I'm trying to connect, I'm serious about my love for Venezia." I balked at the idea of being perceived as yet another tourist. I wanted to fit in, to be part of the city and to live like a local. I was tired of, and embarrassed by, the throngs of people who "did" Venice in less than a day, choking the *calli* in their hundreds.

It was in April 2017 that I managed to find this delightful little apartment overlooking the Grand Canal. I liked its traditional furniture adorned by a few antique pieces, basic facilities, but oh what a wonderful position! I arrived with a girlfriend to celebrate her birthday. She'd never been to Venice before so was still in that state of wonderment when we woke the first morning and watched the traffic on the water: barges delivering supplies, water taxis carrying groups of Japanese tourists bedecked with the obligatory selfie-stick, the *vaporetti*, the blue *carabinieri*, buzzing yellow ambulances, and, of course, the graceful black gondolas. We could have sat all day just watching the activity.

Returning after a day of exploring the city, I sat down with my copy of John Kent's *Venice*, a cleverly-designed little book that illustrates the buildings along each side of the Grand Canal and gives some historical background to the more important of them. It was then that I discovered that our humble abode had a name. Ca' Biondetti.

I cannot write the name without a well of emotion as it has become so special to me. Little did I know that this modest, brick-built house was, at one time, the home of the eighteenth century's greatest female artist, Rosalba Carriera. My discovery was to lead me to unearth the memory of this house and the many illustrious people who had stepped through its door since the year 1700.

Rosalba was 27 years old when she and her family moved to Venice from Chioggia, where she had been born. Ca' Biondetti became the family home on the first of November 1700, and it remained Rosalba's until her death in 1757.

The Carriera family was by no means wealthy. Rosalba's father was a government clerk, her mother a skilled lace-maker. (I too am a lace-maker, so I was thrilled by the connection!) Rosalba had spent her early years designing patterns for her mother's work before diversifying into the art of painting miniatures, an art form that has always fascinated me. The miniatures soon progressed to Rosalba developing into a celebrated pastel portraitist, resulting in the house and family being honored by a visit in 1709 from King Fredrik VI of Denmark, who visited the studio to have his portrait painted. Thus began a catalogue of distinguished sitters as Rosalba's reputation spread throughout Europe. This humble household entertained kings and statesmen, noblemen and women, and countless English gentlemen making the Grand Tour. Artists and writers, singers and musicians, all joined the endless procession of callers across the years.

In 1720 Rosalba was invited to Paris to work at the court, so consequently Ca' Biondetti was left in the capable hands of the family's servants, Elizabeth and Eleanor. Rosalba's godfather popped by to keep an eye on things. He found the kitchen in good order and dropped off some flour and wine. (Callers often commented on the delicious cakes that were served and, on one occasion, a sausage omelet!) I love to imagine the homely gatherings that must have taken place here.

Rosalba returned in 1721 and from then on travelled very little, preferring the security and comfort of her own home. However, in 1728, due to the huge number of commissions, she welcomed into the house Felicità Sartori and her sister Angioletta. Felicità was to become an accomplished pastel portraitist in her own right under the tutelage of Rosalba. She and her sister remained with the family for thirteen years until Felicità left for Dresden when she married.

Rosalba's beloved sister Giovanna died in 1737, followed, the next year, by their mother. Her younger sister Angela returned to the house in 1741 following the death of her husband, but the constant trail of visitors to the studio continued, until tragically, in 1745, Rosalba's sight began to trouble her. Two painful operations failed to rectify the problem caused by cataracts until she gradually became totally blind, a disability that she endured for six years until her death in 1757.

When I sit in the house today, I can only imagine the overwhelming grief that Rosalba must have suffered, being able to hear, but not see, the colorful life outside her window. Prone to depression for much of her life, Rosalba's demise seems inordinately sad, yet the house possesses the most uplifting ambience. On her death the property passed to Angela beyond which there is little evidence of its owners until the Biondetti family carried out extensive renovations.

The property came into its own again when I discovered letters addressed from Ca' Biondetti in the late 1800s written by none other than Henry James. A frequent visitor to Venice, James returned to the city in 1894 to undertake a serious mission: the settlement of his friend Constance Fenimore Woolson's estate. Woolson, another widely acclaimed American author, had rented rooms at Ca' Biondetti whilst seeking a more comfortable house in the city. Yet another artist prone to depression, she had chosen to live in the upper floors of the house as the lantern room in the roof let in light. She had five windows on the canal and apparently spent hours, just as we do, looking at the water-traffic. The upper stories afforded panoramic views of the city and were both light and airy. I assume that the lantern room was Rosalba's studio.

Living below Woolson was a group of ladies from Boston, namely Miss Felton (whose father was President of Harvard) and Miss Lily Norton (daughter of Charles Eliot Norton, Professor of Fine Arts). Opposite them were Miss Huntington and Mrs. Quincy of Boston, whose son was Assistant Secretary of State. How busy the hallway must have been with their chatter!

However, on the tenth of September Woolson moved to Palazzo Semitecolo, (a much larger property, but only a little way down the canal towards the Salute), owned by Lieutenant-General de Horsey. It was here on the twenty-forth of January 1894 that she was found dead on the pavement below, having fallen from a window. Those who knew her well believed her death to have been suicide.

When James left Ca' Biondetti he said goodbye to Venice, ending a long love affair with the city, which he felt had been marred by recent events. I like to imagine this great man sitting at the window here, scribbling notes for his new novel, *The Coxun Fund*, before wandering down the passageway to cross the

Accademia bridge to dine with his friends the Curtises at Palazzo Barbaro.

Not only did Ca' Biondetti attract the likes of Woolson and James (as well as the American ladies), but in 1908 the English aristocrat and socialite Lady Ottoline Morrell and her husband Philip appear in photographs taken at the house: Philip on the balcony, Ottoline peering out of the upstairs window, dressed in her characteristically dramatic wardrobe, or stepping into a gondola at the landing stage.

By 1910 further letters written from Ca' Biondetti emerge. This time the writer is Bertrand Russell, the English philosopher (who began an affair with Ottoline the following year) who is sitting at the window. No doubt it was Ottoline who tipped off Russell about the delightful accommodation that she had discovered.

This unassuming house, its memories and ghosts, has been my passion for much of a year. Just one tiny corner of this enchanting city, yet home, albeit often temporary, to so many renowned people. Sadly my own intimate relationship with Ca' Biondetti will end very soon, as the apartment has been sold, but I imagine that my love affair with this humble place will continue nonetheless. Who knows to whom the new owners will be writing whilst observing the traffic outside their window and listening to the gondoliers serenading the tourists?

As I'm in sympathetic company, I'm going to bravely make a confession. The interior brickwork in the house is so damp in places that there are small areas of brick that are crumbling away. Knowing that I will never have the chance to return to this house, which has come to mean so much to me, I collected a few pieces to keep as a memento. They somehow serve to connect me with the soul of the building.

As for the spritz? I have to confess that I poured my first one into a potted plant when no one was looking, mortified that I had failed the initiation test to appear Venetian. So for me? It's a Bellini every time. *Salute*!

Biography

Jane Mosse was born in Newcastle-upon-Tyne, England. Her first published work was for users of the 2,300 miles of the British Waterways (ironically more canals than Venice, but alas, no gondolas!). She now lives on the island of Guernsey in the Channel Islands with her husband, fellow poet Richard Fleming. She has recently published her first collection of poetry, Guernsey Legends, *which is available from blueormer.co.uk.*

"Lord Byron's Gondolier" by Claudia Oliver

How do you express, in a few short pages, your passion for all that one place is to you? Is it achievable when your subject is a city so old, and so complex, and so vibrant that a thousand books cannot do it justice? If your connection to Venice is, like mine, very personal, how do you convey that to someone who might only see the city as a crowded, expensive tourist trap with a cruise ship complex and a patriotism borne from trying to preserve its dwindling native population? How do you explain to both Venetians and casual visitors alike what it means to come home to somewhere that has never actually been your home, but where your roots are firmly planted historically?

I have found writing about Venice a real struggle because I can barely put into words how it feels every time I return to Venice and immerse myself in an extraordinary world on the water. It has always been relatively easy for me to write about the subject of my connection—my ancestry, and one particular figure who has been immortalized in eighteenth century literary history. But I confess to having spent considerably more time paining over collecting my thoughts on Venice, than actually writing about it. Even now, I am unsure I have done a substantial enough job of trying to explain what Venice means to me. I am not writing in biographical terms here; I am writing about an emotional connection to a place that dwarfs even my unusual origins. Of course, you cannot preach to everyone, and it takes a particular kind of person to see Venice for what it truly is, to feel it in their heart, to understand what being from Venice and being in love with Venice, really is.

The reality is that I am a charlatan by "*Venexiane*" standards. My connection to La Serenissima was realized back in the early 1990s when I discovered that my great-great-great-grandfather had been a gondolier at the Palazzo Mocenigo in the San Samuele district. My first taste of Venice itself, however, came ten years later, when in 2002, by way of a competition entry based on my family tree discovery, I presented a small section of "50 Places to See Before You Die" for the BBC.

The trip, at the height of the tourist season, was a heady whirlwind. For three days we were shepherded by our guide,

Patricia Ann Weston Liani, and our English BBC producer around the usual landmarks with a small Italian film crew in tow. I was acutely and painfully aware that we were behaving like typical tourists, not my favorite guise by any stretch of the imagination. Venice's residents are used to seeing film crews and foreign visitors in their millions, and they are not impressed. I was just one of them, and it didn't sit well with me. We were nothing special. This wasn't the visitor I wanted to be. Even so, this was a free (for me at least) first taste of a place I had only ever dreamed of seeing up close.

We saw the usual tourist traps so that our crew could capture enough footage for the few minutes of screen time we had been allotted on the show. At least I got a free ride in a gondola with "Roberto" and I got up close to the Palazzo Mocenigo from the Grand Canal. Sitting in a real life gondola, I was experiencing one of the oldest professions of the city, in the world even, and I could claim my family as being a part of that skilled set of natives. Gondoliers, however, aren't very impressed by tourists who tell them they are descended from their clan. And the Venetian surname from which I came is barely recognized now except to the older generation of *remèri* and gondoliers.

During that first visit, I only caught a glimmer of the city I really wanted to know and the one I felt I connected with. We stayed at the Casa Verado Hotel near San Marco, where it turned out, quite by coincidence, my cousins were staying exactly the same week. Just hanging out of the window watching the world go by below me was in itself a treat. The canal that ran below the balcony of my bedroom provided the perfect viewing platform to watch gondolas floating past. It encapsulated everything I wanted from my visit.

Just over a year later I was back, but this time I was doing it my way, or at least I thought I was. I am the kind of traveller that wants to avoid tourist traps. In order to find those hidden spots, those places where the locals go, you have to know where to look, and in those formative years I really didn't have a clue about what the city really was. I have had the privilege to visit Venice ten times now, but it is only in the last two, both in 2017 when I travelled alone, that I was really able to connect with the Venice I wanted to be a part of. It was thanks to the final stages of research I was then doing into my family tree, and the connections I had made online during the previous year, that I was finally able to immerse myself in the Venice I love. By then, that research had grown out of all proportion and into a 300-page book, a biography about my Venetian ancestor and his fascinating and famous life. My journey into my family history had been very slow, and it is only in the last two years that I have discovered so much about my ancestor's life, his descendants and ancestors, as well as some of the more minor characters who played an important role in their lives.

My great-great-great-grandfather was Giovanni Battista Falcieri, and he was born on Murano in 1798. When he was 16, Giovanni or "Tita" as he was better known, moved with his parents, two brothers, and sister, from Murano and took up residence as gondoliers to Lucia Mocenigo at the Palazzo Mocenigo on the Grand Canal. Just a few years later the infamous English poet Lord Byron arrived in Venice and rented a level of the Palazzo Mocenigo from Lucia, and Tita became his personal gondolier. That was the beginning of him being launched into history. Without Byron, Tita may have never left Venice in 1820 when he accompanied Byron to mainland Italy and then to Greece where the poet died during the Greek War of Independence in 1824, and I would not be here now. Affections for the main players in this story run deep.

As part of my work I had the challenge of deciphering old Italian baptism, marriage, and death records. And so I decided to learn Italian. I wanted to understand the language myself to enable me to work on the documentation without having to ask for a translator's help. In less than a year I understood enough of the language to be relatively proficient at the basics, and this alone has been pivotal in helping me to connect with Venice on a deeper level. By understanding a little of the culture, the Italian personality of which Tita was standard Venetian, and the language and dynamics of Venetian life, I began to be able to predict my ancestor's behaviours and appreciate his finer qualities. He was passionate, excitable, loyal, and he had a very fiery temper. Five months after I started to self-teach Italian, in 2017, I was back in the city for the first time in ten years and a whole other world opened up to me.

You see, for me Venice isn't about the Piazza San Marco or the Rialto or the Arsenale, although of course those are important historical landmarks. For me it is about eight euro *cicchetti* and an Aperol in a bar tucked away from the prying eyes of the foreign tourist mob. It's about getting lost in back streets without a map, it's about trying my hand at rowing a gondola, or at least a version of it, with the help of Row Venice. It's about heading down the Calle Mocenigo Casa Nuova, touching the crumbling brickwork of the Palazzo Mocenigo as I go, knowing that my ancestors would have walked and talked and stopped here to pass the time with neighbors.

On reaching the end and the little wooden jetty that creaks against the lapping waters of the Grand Canal, I can sit for hours and survey the vast expanse of water that divides the city. I can watch the gondolas as they cross back and forth between the *traghetti* of San Tomà with foot passengers taking a more direct route than the tourist-choked Rialto or Accademia. This *traghetto* is where Tita's father Vicenzo ended his working life in Venice after he retired from the Palazzo Mocenigo. For me, Venice is about taking a *vaporetto* to Murano past the haunting Cimitero, standing on a particular canal side street in the Santo Stefano district and knowing this is where my ancestors were born. This is the earliest point in history that I know we existed. We are here.

Like Tita, who travelled from Italy to Jamaica, Egypt, Albania, Greece, and finally to England in 1832 where he eventually settled, I have wanderlust. I go where fate takes me, and I never settle for long enough to really call anywhere home. I have often remarked how I could live in Venice if the opportunity ever came up. But as Polly Coles discovers in "The Politics of Washing," I know I will never be Venetian. I will never be "one of them."

It doesn't matter what anyone says, of course, because I am descended from Venetian stock and that will always be in my blood. It is why whenever I visit Venice, and as I fly in over the lagoon and strain to catch those first glimpses of the city through the tiny portholes of the plane, as I get off the flight, as I get on the Alilaguna, and as I fix my gaze on the horizon for my first glimpse of the spikes of bell towers and churches as they pierce the haze of the horizon, I feel that longing in my chest that is like falling in love for the first time. Once I have seen my first gondola and heard that first peal of Venetian church bells, I know I am home.

Biography

Claudia is a writer and fashion designer and currently lives in Manchester, UK. Claudia's interest in Lord Byron began when she discovered her g-g-g-grandfather was his gondolier and bodyguard Tita Falcieri. She published her biography of his life A Most Faithful Attendant—The Life of Giovanni Battista Falcieri *in 2014 and a revision is due to be published in 2018. She has contributed to various publications and has appeared on TV and radio in connection with her research. As well as running her own business, Claudia is currently working on a film script about Tita's life.*

"My First Spritz Was a Long Time Ago"
by Cecelia Pierotti

Arriving in Venice always feels new and always feels, well, old. Old in the sense of living a past life or two. While in my late twenties, with a three month Eurail pass in hand and stays in London and Paris behind me, I entered the Santa Lucia train station for the first time with a bit of trepidation. The advice of friends who'd been to Venice before me lingered in my mind, as I wondered whose words I could trust. But as the doors of the station closed behind me that July afternoon, there was a hush in the air (unlike entering the Venice of today). I watched the strange scene of boats silently bobbing on the water. Time stood still as I realized... I could trust my memory. I've been here before and I will surely be here again. My friends and family always wonder if my next trip will be the one where I just stay for good.

I'm obsessed with Venice with a tattoo to prove it. Through the years, I've watched the toll that mass tourism and climate change have taken on this precious and precarious city. Recently it was reported that there were 37 million visitors in Venice in 2017, the highest amount ever. On any given day, there are more tourists than residents. Sadly, the residents don't benefit from this tourism. Blame what you will, the huge cruise ships, the constant flow of day trippers, even Airbnb. The exodus of residents and artisans to the mainland continues. There may be a tipping point (some say it has already reached that point).

The stories that follow take place in the quiet corners of Venice, where if you look deeper you will find so much hope for this threatened city. For instance, this typical day with Ingrid, a friend who was visiting from Germany....

Wandering in Venice 101:

We wanted to go to the Abbess in Cannaregio, out at "the end of Venice." I had been told that they grow flowers there for sale. We couldn't start our exploration without a stop at an intimate neighborhood *ciccheteria*. The very affable proprietor Andrea always greets me as if we are old friends. After enjoying a refreshing Prosecco, a bit of *cicchetti* (Venetian tapas), and chatting, we set out once again. The jewel box of a church the Miracoli was nearby, so we had to stop and admire the treasures within.

From there we both were craving *risotto al mare* (seafood risotto). I remembered an old restaurant that occasionally served the risotto. We crossed a bridge, turned a corner, walked a bit more, and found the restaurant. Happily, we discovered that this dish was on the menu that day. With a fine risotto, a local chardonnay, and lots more conversation under our belts, we figured we were well fortified to try and find the Abbess. Up and away we went, but soon got distracted by the massive Church of San Giovanni e Paolo. We spent the next hour or so marveling at the Bellini and Veronese, the floors, the altars, and the WALLS. Are they painted or are they really brick? (Painted.) The size and wonder of it all is completely daunting and dazzling.

Ingrid and I finally left the cool comfort of the church to return to the warm soup of August and complete our mission to find the Abbess. We succeeded, only to discover that it was closed by this time because we were busy being in Venice!

Pet Care in Venice 101:

For the past several years, I have been housesitting for Frank and Liesl on the island of Giudecca, caring for their dog and cat. Learning animal schedules as well as how doors, keys, the stove and oven, the washing machine, etc., function in an Italian home is always somewhat challenging. Unique to this part of the world is how to hang clothes in the wind from a window several stories high, or to be sure that the furniture on the *altana* (a wooden roof top terrace) is secure, especially when a storm is coming. I dread that a chair might fly off the *altana*, landing on some unsuspecting person below. And while walking the dog India at 7 a.m., I've completely given up trying to cut a "*bella figura*" (Italian for "making a good impression").

Speaking of dog walking, I have had the excitement of taking an ailing dog on a *vaporetto* five times to the local veterinarian. The vets were quite amused by my struggling to describe in broken Italian what was happening. The word "*graffiare*" (to scratch) came in very handy. It was great "fun" to hopefully follow all their directions, three times a day up and down three flights of stairs.

Fortunately, my dear friends Agnieszka and Maciej were visiting and were a great help through it all.

I needed to wash the dog's head with an antibiotic wash purchased at a *farmacia* on the Giudecca. In order to not make a huge mess in the bathroom of the apartment and avoid a certain disapproving neighbor (who acted as if using the garden for anything was highly inappropriate), it was necessary to take India "discreetly" down the stairs. Discretion was a difficult task, however, with a watering can, towels, and three laughing adults in tow. In addition, India needed oral antibiotics purchased at another *farmacia* near the Rialto, the equivalent of a day trip from the Giudecca (remember "Wandering in Venice"). I also had to find "*il cono di vergogno*" (the cone of shame) at yet another location. By the time I found that shop, it was closed for the afternoon.

Undeterred, there was a bar nearby where I was able to enjoy a spritz and await the reopening of that particular shop. No such thing as one stop shopping in Venice! I earned a few residents' stripes that trip.

Venetian Summer Storms 101:

Liz Salthouse and I were invited to the exquisite *palazzo* of Andre and Renaud one muggy summer evening for *aperitivi* (cocktails). Conversation flowed with ease, and drinks turned into dinner and dinner into a late evening. After midnight with fewer boats running, I needed to get from San Marco to Giudecca. Except there was a bigger problem. As our hosts closed the door behind Liz and me, the heavens suddenly opened up. The sky threw a horizontal rain at us that rendered our umbrellas (so proudly remembered in the first place) useless. We ran laughing hysterically across San Marco Square as the sky lit up. Buckets of rain came crashing and dumping down on us to the accompaniment of gale force winds.

The only way to get back to the critters in my care on the Giudecca was by boat. It is really difficult to figure out which boat actually goes from San Marco to the Redentore stop on Giudecca, especially at that hour. Everyone we asked for assistance, in Italian I might add, really seemed to take a bit of delight in sending us to and fro. Perhaps they wanted to witness how much more soaked and frustrated we could get. Liz would not leave me until I could get a boat, or she would take me back to stay in her guest room. I felt the need to persist, however, to find a way back to the animals and not leave them to their own devices overnight.

At this point during the storm, a *vaporetto* had already sunk nearby, and San Marco Square was deserted. I decided to break down and ask a taxi boat driver how much it would cost to get across the Giudecca canal, barely a five-minute ride. "Fifty euros," he declared. NO WAY, I thought to myself .... "Forty?" I meekly countered in Italian and he quipped, "It could be sixty!" (Eeesh, this young man is a pro!) Okay, will wait with the driver and his friend in their little hut and try to eavesdrop on the news of the storm. I did understand the part where he said we should wait "if we want to live," while the winds settled down.

The winds did settle, and the taxi driver beckoned hurriedly for me to join him on his boat. Liz waved me off, watching to make sure we didn't capsize. I held on tightly to my seat on the ride that the young driver called *"cinque minuti di paura"* (five minutes of fear). After the bumpy ride the boat deposited me almost to my door as the heavens calmed down considerably. I was relieved to find the household still in one piece. The animals seemed perfectly happy to see me, as if nothing was wrong with my coming in at that hour looking like a drowned rat. Typical Venetian summer weather with the storms ending as quickly as they begin, and the thunder... but that's another chapter.

Kissing a Relic 101:

When visiting the Church of San Pantalon a couple years ago to gaze at the incredible ceiling, Liz and I stumbled on some sort of a *festa*. There were "priests" with long beards holding receptacles of all types. Women of a certain age were hovering about and singing in beatific harmonies. We determined that it was some sort of Greek or Russian event as they weren't singing in Italian (or Latin). We wandered a bit, but the activities finally piqued our curiosity.

Liz asked a lovely older woman what was happening. "Oh, it is the Feast of San Pantalon, and we are celebrating the relics. Would you like to kiss one?" What?! She was asking a lapsed Catholic and an avowed atheist, neither of whom have a religious bone fragment left in their bodies, to kiss a relic. If we kiss the relics, will we make them explode? Maybe we will burst into flames or be destined to lives of behaving ourselves (the bigger fear). Well, the curiosity and eventual travel attitude of "Why not"? prevailed, and off we went to kiss a silver hand with some sort of fragment in it. At first I actually moved to touch the relic with my fingers, and the priest kindly whispered, "No, kiss it!" and we all survived.

I was humbled reading the story of Saint Pantalon (Saint Pants as Liz and I affectionately like to call him) and his service to those in need. The number of times he DIDN'T succumb to all kinds of horrid attempts at his life was impressive. Liz and I went on with our day, but from then on "kissing the relic" was our call to action when there was something new to try or do!

I have so many more Venetian vignettes to tell. There was the bike ride on the agricultural island of Sant'Erasmo. I had broken my toe prior to that trip, and the rental bike had no brakes. There's the story of a *cicchetti* crawl (going from bar to bar, drinking spritz or Prosecco and eating bites of wonderful this and that). It's a serious business if you do it right, which I did once and survived to talk about it. I've been stopped by the finance police, have marched with WSM (ViVaSan Marco), and watched the Regatta Storica from the Palazzo Benzon. I took part in a documentary on mass tourism and touched the ancient art of bead making. Venetian bells have become the soundtrack of my stays in Venice. The ringing doesn't have a rhyme or reason. It could be 9:23 in the morning on a Tuesday, and there will be bells ringing somewhere.

This crazy, crowded city on water has a profound hold on my heart. If truth be told, Venice is the love of my life. Every time I'm there I feel THIS time was the most special, and the Venetian canal water that courses through my veins just seems to course that much more powerfully. Will the city survive the continual onslaught of mass tourism? I don't have an answer for that. I'm too busy looking closely at the nooks and crannies of day-to-day Venice, and I still see so much life in the "old girl."

Biography

Cecelia is a truly obsessed lover of all things Venetian. She enjoys the luxury of house sitting for friends in Venice every year, walking their dog, and taking language classes. When not in Venice, you can find her in her home violin studio, in Vallejo, California, teaching private students from four years of age through adults, or playing with her trio, Cededa, on her five string electric violin. Enjoying a long career as Vallejo's premier violin teacher, she continues to look forward to yearly breaks in her home away!!

Her website is: vallejoviolinstudio.com

On Facebook: Cecelia Pierotti, Vallejo Violin Lessons, Cededa

"You Have to Get Lost" by Luisella Romeo

Can you really fall in love with a city you didn't choose? As Venice is the city where I live and where my family has lived for generations, it may feel hard to imagine I could fall in love with it. You can love it, but falling in love is, as we know, a different story. It feels incestuous, something that does not come spontaneously. And yet, it happened.

I recall memories of me as a young child falling in love with Venice's water. In the winter night, on a *vaporetto*, leaving the island of Giudecca, I recall the bubbling dark water because of the propeller accelerating. But also the calm, flat surface of the lagoon's water when rowing with my grandfather behind the Giudecca on our blue and white boat, a traditional typical *sandolo*. And the water of the sea, at the Lido, where I loved spending my summer holidays, where clams hid in the sand, and tiny grey crabs climbed the rocks at the dams or by the lighthouse.

Not to mention *acqua alta*, which sounds dramatic, but in the eyes of a child it can be fun to see the city streets covered in water. So jumping from one doorstep to the other to keep my feet dry, or being carried on the shoulders of somebody who had the clever idea to wear rubber boots and saved me....

If the water presence in the city made me fall in love with Venice, I am aware there is one more issue involved in this romance. If you were born in a place like Venice, which everyone says is unique, that there is no other place like it, would you sincerely realize how special the place is? Or just take it for granted? And admit, yes, it is a beautiful city, but can you still see its beauty and feel fascinated? Or have you grown used to it?

I strongly believe you cannot get used to this beauty. Indeed, I think anyone born here can develop love or hate for this city. For several reasons. But we tend to grow into incurable lovers of beauty. Aesthetically attentive. Sophisticated and demanding. Searching for creative solutions for everyday life, loving veneer, used to a contaminated beauty deriving from a history of a mix of cultures, styles, ideas, and physical contact.

Venice is a city of no purity, rather a city where diversity prevails. In a way, you can say Venice does not exist or you can find a bit of Venice anywhere you go. If you try to narrow down the narration of Venice to some elements, you are certainly missing something or eluding one of its facets. You can see the city in too many different perspectives to describe it as a whole. What follows then is my incomplete list!

Venice is a labyrinth. You easily get lost. Who hasn't said so? Everyone does! Many will tell you that this is the pleasure about Venice. That you have to get lost. This is the way to really see the city. Discover its hidden corners, explore the secrets of the city, unveil its authentic beauty. If you don't get lost, you have not seen Venice. A mantra, but all true.

But let me tell you what it is like for someone whose profession is to know every single corner and to be a live GPS, i.e., a tourist guide arranging itineraries in Venice *and* living in Venice. The day I took my father around Castello to reach the waterfront for New Year's midnight fireworks, avoiding all the crowded streets and he exclaimed, "How did you find these streets?!" I realized what had happened. I have reached the point I cannot get lost in Venice. Even my father, born and raised in Venice, knew less than I did. And I felt sad: I do want to still get lost in Venice!

To be honest, I am sure there are corners where I have not been yet, and I cherish them, as the last chocolate candy that you don't want to eat too soon: if you eat it, the pleasure is gone. But it feels like a red fish swimming in a fishbowl, because I know where these corners are.

But don't misunderstand me. I am not saying that the fun is over for me as I know the labyrinth. On the contrary, I love Ariadne's thread because it allows for a lot of fun, especially because I know where each *calle* takes me.

First of all, the labyrinth helps me think. When you drive, you think about where you are going, you drive carefully (hopefully), and you pay attention to what you are doing. When you know where you are in Venice, you walk around, choosing alternative routes because you want to avoid the tourists' crowds or just because you want to get to see that detail again, well... and in the meanwhile you can let your thoughts distract you. You can think. So the labyrinth is there to help me walk and think, enjoy feeling lost in my reveries. Without any fear of a car accident. Which, you will agree, is a plus, both physically and economically. Recently, I have grown used to checking my smartphone notifications while walking. But I am trying hard to get rid of this habit, as it prevents me from looking at the city… and it may bring me to uncomfortable situations, such as stepping on some poop left by a dog (and not collected by its owner) or stumbling on some steps or falling in a canal!

The labyrinth, however, helps me also meet real people. Just by chance. When you drive, you don't meet anyone. Unless you crash against somebody's car. Oh, well. But what happens when I am not working is that I meet someone and start talking to them. They go in one direction, I may go the other direction, but the labyrinth allows me to do something that is really great. It helps me find a detour! An alternative route is always there as long as you know the labyrinth well enough. "Are you going there…? I see, well, I can walk with you for a while as I am not exactly going in that direction, but I can get that far and then you turn and I turn…" or: "If you come this way, you can still get there where you are heading, but at least we can share some of the itinerary together and talk…?" So I detour, you detour too, but eventually we will still go in the right direction, reach our goals and… we will have had time to chat.

I missed Venice when I lived abroad or simply on the mainland. Sure, would you prefer the damp fog that gets in your bones to the lovely sunny weather of California? No, I would not. Would you prefer the densely urbanized, almost claustrophobic city streets to the open green hills of any countryside? No, I would not. Would you prefer to carry your heavy groceries in a shopping cart up and down several bridges or use a comfortable car and its trunk? I would not. I loved big towns, like London, the exhilarating feeling of knowing no one. And yet, I missed Venice.

So I am happy to be here. Surrounded by incredible history. Unique art. Crazy light that changes at any season and any moment, reflecting from different sources. Which, as I love photography, leaves me constantly surprised. And I love the slow pace, which, unlike what one might think, is apparently a sign of efficiency.

Sure. To work in tourism and to love Venice tears me apart and is not easy. The cons of mass tourism affect Venice, often getting the worst out of the residents and of the tourists, at the same time. In fact, I would like to tell anyone visiting Venice that you will never experience Venice as if you were a resident, even when you try hard to. Give it up. It will not work. As anywhere else. We are all tourists

157

when we visit. On the other side, I know it's hard to ask residents to accept over 20 million visitors taking pictures of you when you shop groceries or when you row a boat, or simply when a water ambulance is taking you to hospital.

But the meeting ground beyond the conflict exists. And it can be beautiful. I learned this from a young child. He and his friends were playing in a *campo* in Venice with a yellow ball. Then my client, taken by enthusiasm, joined them, playing with them and she kicked the ball with lots of energy. In the wrong direction. The ball fell miserably into the canal. The current started taking the ball away from all the kids desperately looking at it while it moved slowly, farther and farther, floating on the dark water of the canal. My client was so upset. She looked at me, looked at the boy and said, "I am ready to pay for a new ball, I am soooo sorry!" The boy looked at her and said, "No, I don't want the money, but you have to apologize to the owner of the ball," a younger girl, say seven years old standing next to him, in tears. So the lady apologized and the kids went to look for a different ball to keep on playing.

So Venice is also this. How can't you love it?

Biography

Luisella Romeo has been a registered tourist guide in Venice since May of 2000, when she was officially certified by the Regione Veneto.

Throughout all these years she has been a member of the Association of Registered Tourist Guides in Venice and of the National Association of Tourist Guides in Italy. She regularly runs tours in Italian, English, and German. Since 2015 she has been involved in the Best Venice Guides project aimed at promoting high quality tourism by creating a network of local professional tourist guides and the excellence of Venice, its museums, and its art jewels with a focus on alternative routes.

Born and raised in Venice with her family, after graduating at the University in Venice Ca' Foscari in Foreign Languages and Literatures, she had the chance to travel and study abroad. She was granted a scholarship by the University of California at Berkeley and received a travel grant from the Fulbright program. For a few months she also worked at the Fraunhofer Institut in Darmstadt on a project about multimedia databases and art.

She has always loved art and history. She loves photography, modern and contemporary art, Jewish history. Crafts, local economy. For years she has been involved in projects aiming at supporting the local history and contemporary life.

She loves what she does because, as she says: "I love meeting people from all over the world and confront myself with different perspectives and viewpoints. My key is that the labyrinth of Venice is a crossroads of human stories to narrate. And I love my job: I hope you can feel the passion for it when we discover Venice together!"

She lives in Venice, in Cannaregio, with her husband and two cats.

l.romeo@seevenice.it
WEB + Blog: seevenice.it
M +39 349 0848 303
FB SeeVenice Guided Tours by Luisella Romeo
Twitter See Venice Tours @luisella_romeo
Instagram @luisella_romeo

"Coming Home to Venice" by Elizabeth Salthouse

All of a sudden there was a flurry of activity. Hands unceremoniously man-handled me off the plastic waiting room chair onto a trolley. And then everything went black. Until the cannula was inserted. That stung like a bee, but then I've never been a fan of needles. Wide awake again, I began to take in my surroundings. Pristine white walls enclosed a room of medical paraphernalia flooded by soft sunlight. Staff fussed around me, checking vital signs. And an overwhelming sense of calm surrender washed over me. I knew I was safe, and I couldn't think of anywhere I'd rather be than here: at home, in Venice.

Once the drip kicked in, the wonderful medical staff at Venice's Ospedale Santissimi Giovanni e Paolo quickly brought color back to my pallid cheeks. And, happy at last that I wasn't going to faint for a third time, they set about fixing my rather trivial broken finger. I'm not usually this much of a drama queen—honestly—I blame a stomach bug from a weekend away!

Thinking back, that trip to the Pronto Soccorso emergency room does sound rather intense. And it's a great story to tell friends who shake their heads in horror asking if I wasn't frightened being ill, on my own, and speaking in a second language. If I'm honest though, I remember it all very positively.

The doctor and surgeon, for example, both had a lovely paternal bedside manner, urging me with a wink to take better care of myself. The nurses' soft, tender hands took real care of their ashen patient despite my gibberish Italian. The porter was a sweetheart, pushing me hither and thither in a wheelchair for blood tests and X-rays, anxious that I didn't collapse again. And one lovely local lady waiting patiently to have her leg X-rayed even insisted that I, the interloper, must go first—I didn't understand her explanation, but I thanked her nonetheless. It all reminded me of the fundamental goodness of people. I couldn't say *"grazie"* enough.

But we're jumping ahead.

Venice isn't my natural birthplace. The journey to this place had taken years. And the story started much more sedately. Cue wibbly wobbly time-travel effects and a flourish of harp music ...!

Curiously there were no indications that day, years before, that my life had taken a momentous turn. No fireworks, no earthquake, no parade. It was an ordinary Saturday afternoon in northern Britain. The sun was valiantly burning through fluffy white clouds, the streets were packed with shoppers, and I was heading out to get a birthday present for a friend.

So far, so normal.

I must have spent over an hour perusing the shelves of the bookshop—my go-to for gifting inspiration. I'd found three books for myself—they're a bit of an obsession—but still had no present. And there was only one section left to check; I really needed something to leap into my hands before the shop doors shut. So I started at A and slowly worked my way across the pristine spines of the biographies nestled at the back of the shop.

The usual celebrity names popped up. Writers, actors, singers, cooks, and musicians all clamored for my business, but none of them piqued any interest so I carried on.

A little book by Joseph Grimaldi, Britain's famous eighteenth century clown, found its way into the pile under my arm. It looked a fascinating memoir by a funny little man.

On I skimmed until another tome caught my eye.

It was ten times as long as Grimaldi's and twice the price to boot. But something drew me to its spartan, black and white spine. The front cover's sensual painting of a half dressed Renaissance couple in flagrante added to the allure. But it was the name of the author that sealed the deal.

Giacomo Girolamo Casanova, Chevalier de Seingalt.

I never did get a book for my friend. As soon as I got home I opened Casanova's memoirs, eagerly devouring the early years of his life. That book went everywhere despite being heavy as a brick. It came to work so I could immerse myself in canals and Casanova over lunch. It came to the dentist waiting room and the hairdresser. And its tissue-thin pages are bookmarked with a boarding card to Siena, a train ticket from London, and a postcard of Milan as a testament to our travels, too.

As the pages turned, Giacomo journeyed to Padua and back, explored his hometown and beyond, and opened the doors to the daily life of Venetians in greater minutiae than anyone had ever done. He wrote of his gambling and his losses. He documented his travels and friends. He described the meals with which he seduced his ladies, cataloguing each course and cost in detail. He discussed his wardrobe, the silks and threads that adorned his unusual, statuesque 6-foot frame. And he, of course, talked of his lovers, using initials in a delightfully gentlemanly fashion to spare their blushes.

The book was easy to read, split into short chapters sometimes by the day, week, or a specific episode in Casanova's life. It was easy to dip in and out, staying for just a chapter whilst waiting for the bus or greedily polishing off several as the clouds flew past below my holiday flight.

And the more I read, the more I wanted to know, and the more I needed to see the places described. Did they still exist? Would I be able to find them 250 years later? A trip was definitely in order. And serendipitously I was learning Italian at evening class so I could test my nascent language skills on an unsuspecting shopkeeper or two!

Not even Casanova's 1,500-page memoirs prepared me for what I found.

Sure, I'd seen glossy photos of Venice online. And I'd read the guidebook, too. But as the Alilaguna airport waterbus gently chugged across the lagoon and around the eastern tip of Sant'Elena, I caught my first glimpse of St. Mark's bell tower rising against the cobalt blue sky. And I realized why Casanova hated being exiled. The lagoon city is simply breathtaking.

The next four days were a whirlwind affair chasing Casanova through the streets from convent to casino, boudoir to bedroom. I was thrilled to discover my hotel, the Monaco & Grand Canal, had once been a gambling casino and salon where the legendary scallywag had chanced his arm with the card tables and the ladies. From there it was just a short distance to Giacomo's birthplace on a tiny alley off a side street in the *sestiere* of San Marco. It was hard to find with only a flimsy tourist map and the briefest of clues on which to work. But for some reason I was determined to stand in the street where he once walked and to touch the walls that once sheltered him.

From there I zigzagged through his adolescence, tracked his move to San Polo, and located his midnight trysts. He was everywhere—in the Florian coffee house, at the Malibran Theater, in the Rialto fruit market, in Campo San Polo, in the Doge's Palace, on

Murano, and in the churches and *palazzi* dotted across the city. I was in such heaven uncovering the delights of Venice, both old and new, that I decided to extend my trip by another three days, much to the hotel manager's amusement. He clearly thought I was another mad tourist, so I did the tourist thing and went out to eat.

I tucked into *tramezzini*, delicious Venetian sandwiches swollen with filling. Scoffed mouthwatering *cicchetti*, Venice's tapas-style bites. Passed a day exploring Murano, marveling at the deft skills of the glass blowers and bead stringers, drooling over the pastries in the next door family bakeries. Cleared a plate of *sarde in saor*, mopping the tangy juices with warm, fresh bread. And chomped on half a dozen oysters fresh from the Rialto fish market. *Si mangia bene a Venezia*—one eats well in Venice!

All too soon it was my final day, and Venice had saved the best for last.

A dense sea fog descended. Misty tendrils embraced the palaces, creeping stealthily along canals. A thick miasma muffled the clanking of moored boats. Soft cloud fell over low bell towers, church domes, and one entire side of the Grand Canal. And gondolas bobbing in front of the Doge's Palace took on an amazing midnight blue tint as an eerie sapphire hue was cast across the city. It was a magical sight bringing tears to my eyes so, after dinner, I took myself for one last drink to raise a toast to the town and the trip.

Eating or drinking alone is one of the loneliest things to do when travelling, so I always take a book or notepad to deflect any stares. That last night I tucked my trusty Moleskin and favorite fountain pen into my bag to write my diary whilst supping a Bellini. And I didn't have far to trek as Harry's Bar, famous drinking hole, old haunt of Ernest Hemingway and inventor of the Bellini, was just three paces across the alleyway.

Despite the empty streets, the tiny bar was humming. Every table was taken, so I clambered onto a bar stool ear-wigging as the barkeep regaled us with stories of classic combinations and long-lost cocktails. Within minutes a table became free, so I ordered a second cocktail whilst I finished writing my diary.

Unexpectedly, the manager appeared at my side to ask if I'd eaten. I had, thank you, I replied. But had I had dessert, he countered? Well, actually, no....

"Wait there, I have just the thing for you."

Few drinkers realize Harry's has a rather classy dining menu; I'd already admired the delicious *profumo* of the seafood risotto floating across from the next table. It is also a little pricey, so when a plate of four mini desserts appeared, I was anxious. Ah, what the hell.

The sugary sliver of lemon meringue pie slid down very nicely. A rich chocolate tart followed quickly after. My favorite was the vanilla cream cake, but the moist chocolate gateau was excellent, too. I cleared the plate!

As the evening drew to a close, couples began to wend their way home, and I nonchalantly asked for the bill. It came to over €35 but didn't include the food. Very odd.

Before I could query the mistake, the manager asked whom I was I writing my article for, which publication would it be in? The penny dropped! I'd been erroneously promoted from tourist to food critic, and the desserts were on the house!

As the *motoscafo* taxi flew across the lagoon back to the airport the next morning, I made a decision: one day before I died I would live in Venice. I had never wanted to live anywhere else than my hometown before; I was a real homebody and always enjoyed returning home as much as going on an adventure. But that afternoon, as I flew out over the island patchwork, I had a "wish in a suitcase," as Italians say. One day....

Five years later almost to the day, I was made redundant from my office job of 22 years. I was sad that a chapter was ending, but it was the kick up the backside I needed. So I packed my life into a suitcase, gave the house keys to my friend, and set off on a £40 one-way ticket to La Serenissima.

I'd given myself a year off to travel the length of Italy from north to south, starting with six wonderful weeks in a rented apartment in Venice. It was a dream come true, and six weeks quickly turned to twelve. Which grew another month. Then three more before finally deciding to just stay the whole year.

And then, of course, that became two!

Nine years on from that ordinary Saturday in England, I'm still not finished with Venice—I don't think I ever will be—although these days I'm back in the UK.

I still find it hard to explain what drew me to make Venice my home. It was a need, an ache, an imperative tugging me closer and closer as if a string were tied around my heart. It was simply essential I live there to tread the streets once walked by Casanova and Hemingway and Titian and Palladio down through the centuries.

Initially I fell in love with Casanova and his rose-tinted illusion. In the end I fell madly for the lagoon city, warts and all. From its over-tourism and unbearable summer humidity that make knees sweat to the mundane weekly *supermercato* shop. From the eerie mid-winter pea-soupers to the lush green hidden gardens and chats with traditional artisans. From the tempestuous thunderstorms that rattle the fabric of the city to the secret short cuts or nod-and-wink wine prices for those in the know. Or simply standing at the bar with a spritz, a handful of *cicchetti*, and a gaggle of friends all chatting over each other. I love it all—all except the cruise ships, that is—and moving to Venice was the best decision I've ever made as now I have two homes!

Biography

Liz is a freelance travel writer and blogger who has as many tales to tell as she has Italian handbags. She lived in Venice for two blissful years after reading Casanova's diaries and now splits her time between the UK and Italy. She writes about festivals, old traditions, and little known attractions and is happiest chatting with friends over a glass of Hugo and a plate of cicchetti *to share.*

Website: *dreamdiscoveritalia.com*
Facebook: *facebook.com/DreamDiscoverItalia/*
Twitter: *twitter.com/d_d_italia*
Instagram: instagram.com/dreamdiscoveritalia/

"An Imperfect Instant of Bliss in the Campo"
by Scott Stavrou

It's easy to fall in love with Venice. People have been doing it for many centuries. My wife and I were not unique in that regard. There are those who have even fallen in love with Venice and managed to simply go on with their lives.

But the love of Venice is a powerful idea. And great ideas dream of being made manifest. Just like those that stirred the first people who dreamed of a different life and created Venice in a place where no city belonged. And when the idea of something transcends the ordinary and enters into extraordinary, it demands your attention.

Like everyone else, we had our own idea of Venice and it was one we wanted more of in our lives. Our simple ideal of life in Venice had been picked at and played with until it transformed into an infatuation that demanded to be yielded to.

In the misty borders between dream and reality, if one is fortunate or impetuous enough, you find that it's time to act or forever risk losing your chance to make your dreams come true.

There's a lot of in-between in Venice, floating as it does precariously on the misty borders of land and sea, dream and reality. Like Venice itself, we found ourselves in-between things. We were in-between youthful impetuousness and the grown-up acceptance of adulthood and its demands. We had met while traveling Europe and then pretended to be real grown-ups. Got engaged, married, moved back home to America. We settled down, started a business, bought a house. We did all this because it seemed what we were supposed to do, what we were supposed to want.

These things that we'd acquired were what we believed we were supposed to want. They were, it seemed, the very things that real grown-ups were expected to have. But when we looked around at the tangible trappings of the lives we'd built, they felt like exactly that to us: trappings. We wanted more. Or to be more accurate, we wanted less. Less obligation, less convention, less mundanity; in short: less reality. The recommended requisites of real life and convention had been tried, tested, and found wanting. And left us wanting something else.

As we increasingly did more of our business online, we found ourselves more and more looking around at the things that comprised our American lives of cozy but cold convention and becoming eager early embracers of the enticing new idea that we could work anywhere.

Which brought us to the idea of Venice.

After all, what better place in the world to remedy the ills of too-much reality than Venice, a place that positively defied all definitions of reality? Few places are further removed from the regular reality of the real world. Venice has always been something "other": not quite land, not quite sea, not quite dream, not quite reality.

But what we wanted was Venice. And once we let the possibility of moving to Venice tantalize us, it demanded to be yielded to. And because, at the time, the dollar was strong in comparison to the euro, we found that then we could rent an apartment in Venice for less than the cost of our monthly mortgage on our small California house. And so we rented out our house and rented a small apartment in the Dorsoduro that actually cost us less than being tethered to a life we weren't ready for.

And so we packed up some of our things, got the necessary paperwork for our two beloved dogs, and boarded a plane. Moving is never easy, moving abroad, more challenging, still. Moving abroad with dogs to an unseen apartment had its own challenges.

We arrived at Piazzale Roma, entering beautiful Venice through its less-than-beautiful busy back door.

Moving into a Venetian apartment with several large bags, dog carrier crates, and two dogs in tow was not the most straightforward endeavor. But many things in Venice are not straightforward.

We had too many things and too much stuff to even consider the long walk and were ready to splurge for one of the sleek wooden *motoscafo* boats that waited there, but none of the elegant watercrafts were eager to take us with the dogs and rather cumbersome cargo. We asked around and eventually, beyond the elegant polished mahogany lines of the *motoscafi*, we located a squat, flat, black barge with a two drivers dressed alike in dingy work overalls that spoke some halting English and most importantly knew the address in the Dorsoduro and agreed to haul us and our meager menagerie directly to the door.

169

It was a rugged and workaday affair—they and us were equally at odds with the elegant backdrop of Venice and Italian *moda* all around us, and still it seemed fitting and proper to the ramshackle approach we'd taken to the move. Not for us the *motoscafo* of the beautiful people, but then we were poignantly not beautiful people despite being surrounded by some of the most beatific setting and scenery in the world. We were eager to dive into the idea of what the "real Venice" might be like, and for us and our hectic move, the squat and ungainly barge was the perfect entry.

The driver handily helped us stow our bags and burdens on the barge, and with some unseemly cajoling, we finally managed to convince the dogs to step off of the safety of the firmament of *terraferma* and onto the floating barge, though they were clearly none-too-eager to sample yet another new mode of transportation, and we set off on the barge into the winter workaday dusk of Venice through the small canals and then out onto the large Canale della Giudecca.

The winter wind swept in chill and bracing from off the wider expanse of the lagoon as the barge chugged along past the cargo ships and containers of the port on the left and the outline of the Giudecca on the right then motored alongside the ochre-colored *palazzi* that lined the *fondamenta* of the Zattere before it turned lugubriously up the small Rio San Trovaso canal and took us past the dim outline of the out of place-looking wooden Alpine *squero* where sat the evocative and serene black silhouettes of gondolas that were being repaired and refurbished for the next season, past the small grassy portion of the *campiello* in front of the large Chiesa di San Trovaso and then moored along the *fondamenta* that lies before our rental apartment just by a small arched stone bridge that spanned the twelve feet or so of the small canal.

While my wife took the dogs up for a first viewing of the third-floor apartment, the kindly bargemen offered to help with the baggage. While one of them and myself carried what we could up the stairs, the second generous helper placed himself and the remaining bags in the small elevator for easy carriage. And when the elevator got stuck in-between floors, after the consternation of a surprise meeting of our new neighbors, we hadn't expected to hear the sirens of two boats of Venice's firemen, the *Vigili del Fuoco*.

Ten firemen zealously debated and opined about the problem of the poor man stuck in the elevator and swarmed around the stairs and petted our dogs in the apartment. And once they solved the small problem of the stuck elevator and saved the day, they were off with enthusiastic *ciaos* and warm well-wishes for our first Venetian winter, still expressing mild shock and dismay that we'd chosen to leave California for Venice.

Everyone has their own idea of paradise. And most frequently, those paradisiacal ideas are elusive and faraway.

Not so in Venice. When you've loved and dreamed of Venice for a long while and have just moved to an apartment in the Dorsoduro, paradise is all around you.

The first weeks were of settling in. The many machinations of obtaining the first private residence broadband Internet connection in the whole of the *sestiere* Dorsoduro. Letting the dogs gloriously and safely explore the car-free *calli* and *campi*. Tossing a Frisbee to our energetic bird dog in the small park by the squero in front of Chiesa di San Trovaso and enjoying the many choruses of *"bravo, bravo"* each time he gracefully snagged the soft Frisbee out of the air, teaching his many new fans how to throw a Frisbee for the first time.

Living with a high-energy dog, we were fortunate that our apartment was nestled just behind one of Venice's rare small public patches of grass. His enthusiastic chasing and retrieving of the Frisbee became a much-appreciated and applauded regular spectacle.

There was the selecting of our favorite cafes and *cicchetti* spots, our favorite just across the small canal in front of the apartment, where even in the bitter cold of a Venetian winter, early evenings would find us joining the locals for a shadow of wine, *un'ombra* and some delicious Venetian delicacies.

There was the business of getting to know the local produce man who sold his wares from his barge on the Rio San Barnaba. Choosing a favorite *gelateria*. Marveling at the taste and the selection. Allowing these small but delicious pleasures to become part of a new and magical routine.

After some weeks, the Venetians begin to realize that you're not just a part of the immemorial ebb and flow of transitory tourists, but attempting to live your life among them. You slowly notice a bit of their reserve fades. You see both relief and acceptance of the fact that you're no longer just a tourist.

When you take your dogs out with you for a *passeggiata* in the campo, you start to get nodded at with recognition, receive more ciaos, *va benes*, and *buona seras*. Your dogs know which of the kindly elderly women in the *campo* make a habit of carrying dog biscuits in their pockets and run up and sit for them to earn a treat and a pat.

When on a rare clear sunny afternoon in January, you pass by your favorite little *trattoria* in the Campo Santa Margherita, the kindly owner nods. Sit down, he beckons. No, you say, gesturing at your dogs cavorting in the *campo*. Fine, bring the dogs, he invites.

Being from San Francisco, the dogs are not much accustomed to lingering in cafes. They are not yet continental canines. But the day is glorious and he's so gracious and a small plate of *sarde in saor* and a shadow of wine, *un'ombra,* sounds pretty irresistible.

So you sit down and temporarily tether the dogs to the small table and eat and drink in the rare winter sunshine of the *campo* and all is right with the world.

Right up until you accidentally drop a piece of bread on the ground and a few cawing pigeons fearlessly strut over to snatch the bread and your Frisbee-hunting bird dog remembers his long-forgotten instincts and barks and bolts and there's a small catastrophic crash of cutlery and late-lunch detritus and his leash pulls out the table in his eagerness of chase.

And as you round up your ill-trained dog and calm his ineluctable instincts and attend to cleaning up the mess, the kindly proprietor disdains your apologies and offers of extra euros.

And so you let the dog free to stroll the stones of the *campo* as he instructs, and you sit back down in the waning sunshine and order a spritz and marvel at the timeless and magical spectacle of everyday Venetian life as it unfolds around you.

And you realize that for this time, this *campo* is your backyard, your neighborhood, no longer your dream, and you start to understand and appreciate that Venice and the love of Venice will be a part of your life forever. Even if only for these sweet special months, your dream has become where you live.

Biography

Scott Stavrou is the author of Losing Venice, *a novel (2018). He has lived and worked as a writer in San Francisco, Venice, and Prague, and he and his wife presently live on a small Greek island where he also teaches Creative Writing. He has written fiction and nonfiction for numerous publications and was awarded a PEN International Hemingway Prize for short fiction.* Losing Venice *is his second book.*

ScottStavrou.com
Twitter: @WriteAwayEurope (6,000 followers)
Medium: medium.com/@ScottStavrou

"The More I Go to Venice..." by Katia Waegemans

When I plan a trip to Venice, the moment I look forward to mostly is the feeling when I descend from the escalators at the Marco Polo airport to the waterfront. I always hold my step to take a deep breath of the Venetian air. The intense joy in this split second makes me realize I'm back at my home away from home.

I usually arrive with a late flight, hence my transfer in the water taxi is in the dark of night. This allows me to put my mind to rest and leave all the stress and worries behind. For me, Venice equals peace and quiet. Even on crowded days, the sheer beauty of the city and the silence thanks to the lack of cars seem to absorb the buzz of locals and tourists. Wandering around Venice, I feel at home in the maze of the city, and I forget everything around me. I could easily bump into a friend, or George Clooney for that matter, without even noticing.

My addiction to Venice started in 2004, even though I had been to the city several times beforehand. It was the year I fell in love with Jef. For our first romantic trip together, we chose Venice. Since then, our common love for the city has been a determining element in our own love story. It even culminated in our wedding in Palazzo Cavalli in Venice. Every time we visit, we fall in love again, with each other and with La Serenissima, as we were on that first trip. This is a perfect reason to return time and time again.

It's hard to define what makes Venice so addictive. I have been so many times, in different seasons, with and without crowds, and I'm still surprised by the *palazzi*, the canals, the *calle*, and all the small details that together define what Venice is. Many people don't understand why I return so often to the same city. Just the other day, even my sister wondered if I had seen something new on my last visit. The "problem" is actually the opposite. The more I go, the more I realize how much I haven't seen yet. My list of things to visit always becomes longer instead of shorter.

The cultural heritage, in the widest sense of the word, in Venice is endless. For every trip, I have to define my priorities on what I really want to see. At the moment, the historic gardens are high on my list, as are the small islands such as Sant'Erasmo (an agricultural island which is considered to be the vegetable garden of Venice) or

San Lazzaro degli Armeni (a former leper colony which now houses an Armenian monastery with a stunning library). My list also includes the exquisite *palazzi* such as Palazzo Grimani (a remarkable Renaissance building which was originally the residence of Doge Antonio Grimani) or Palazzetto Bru Zane (the former *casino* of the Zane family which hosts now the Centre de musique romantique française), and ... I could go on forever. Some of these have been on my list for a while, but there always seems to be something better or more intriguing. Every conversation about Venice and every article I read triggers my inspiration for a series of new ideas that I want to discover. It's a never-ending story.

One of the reasons that I always find something new to explore is the fact that I love art and especially contemporary art. I easily spend a few hours to visit a good exhibition at, for instance, Punta della Dogana. Considering the huge number of museums and exhibitions in Venice, you can understand that it consumes a lot of my time even with only one exhibition per year per museum. In an attempt to find the right balance with the cultural heritage as such, I do skip many of these temporary activities. I am also a very big fan of the Biennale, both the Art Biennale and the Architecture Biennale. The advantage of these events is the fact that several pavilions are spread across the city. Not only does this allow me to discover these *palazzi*, but it also brings me across all the *sestieri* and even the lagoon islands.

Another guilty pleasure is everything related to books and bookstores. I love to take the time to browse through novelties and classics in a bookshop. On my last visit, I was happy to discover two new stores (Sulaluna in Cannaregio and Marco Polo Libreria on Giudecca) that I really loved. I'm sure I will spend more time there in the future. The original settings of Acqua Alta in Castello and of the boat with books on Campo San Barnaba in Dorsoduro are also great places to forget about time and browse through books to discover the unexpected.

The most important element of Venice is of course the people who live in the city or consider the city their second home. Over time, I have gotten to know many of them (and several are also part of this book), some only online but others also on my frequent visits to Venice. The openness and generosity of the Venetians is just amazing. For example, one of my blog followers introduced me to

Margherita and Stefano, who run the Cantiere Manin on Giudecca. Without knowing me, they took the time to show me around their workshop and share their passion for the "*pali da casada*." These colorful poles in front of *palazzi* and hotels along the canals are an intrinsic part of the skyline and the architecture of the city. Even though every visitor takes at least one picture of a *pala*, little has been written about this topic. This type of experience cannot be found in any guidebook, so these unique encounters make my visits to Venice memorable. There are also the impromptu encounters with other local entrepreneurs and artisans who love to talk about their activity. I had, for instance, the pleasure to meet the team at Smallcaps and Arianna of Plum Plum Creations in their respective workshops. They are both active in artisanal printing, but with a totally different approach. Smallcaps specializes in screen printing, while Plum Plum Creations focuses on linocuts and etching. These meetings always leave a lasting impression and make every trip unique.

A large part of my visits is spent just wandering around, following my intuition at every corner or my eyes that notice a detail somewhere. To some, these might seem like ordinary streets. However, I like to discover small statues on a façade, a first floor that is wider than the ground floor, or special doorknobs and wonder what they symbolize. It brings me to unexpected locations where I can relax and enjoy the peace and quiet, ideally on a terrace with a good glass of spritz.

If I try to summarize my reasons of addiction to Venice, I can't name a specific landmark or reason. It's a combination of love and romance, beautiful surroundings, intriguing art and literature, fascinating people, and above all peace and quiet.

When I plan a trip to Venice, the moment I dread most is when I get back in my car at the airport in Belgium and hit the road. Luckily, this is also the time to plan my next trip and turn this whole story into a vicious circle.

Biography

Katia Waegemans is a Belgian citizen who loves Venice and travels several times per year to the city. To share her passion with other frequent visitors, she started her travel blog The Venice Insider *in December 2015.*

Website: theveniceinsider.com
Facebook: facebook.com/theveniceinsider
Twitter: twitter.com/TheVeniceInsider
Instagram: instagram.com/the_venice_insider

"First Smitten" by Vonda Wells

I am having a little love affair with Venice. This is my response to the many who question why I return to Venice again and again. Yes, I am in love with a city. It's the most accurate way I can describe the way I feel. As women we are all familiar with the notion of love and of course the intense euphoria of falling in love. It happens differently every time. Sometimes it comes from a developing admiration. Sometimes it's love at first sight. Sometimes it occurs softly and sweetly. Sometimes we perilously and helplessly fall in love. And sometimes, it hits us out of nowhere like a ton of bricks.

I will never forget the moment I realized I was smitten. My husband and I were on our first trip to Italy with a tour group. We had seen the beautiful and amazing sights in Rome, Florence, and many places in between, and I had been eagerly looking forward to the final two days we would spend in Venice. I already knew I would like it there, having always been enchanted by the idea of the magical floating city where streets are canals, and cars are boats. The tour group had arranged hotel rooms on the mainland, and after settling in, we arrived, by *vaporetto* (waterbus), at the actual island of Venice after dark. My first sight of her was in the soft pink glow of her tinted streetlights. So it was that I began to take in her beauty one *palazzo*, bridge, and cobblestoned step at a time. One by one she gradually revealed her charms to me, and so while my visit was absolutely delightful, I did not experience that overwhelming love at first sight as many do. During our visit we shopped, ate, toured, and thoroughly enjoyed the city, just as I had anticipated. It was the perfect ending of a magnificent trip.

As our final night was drawing to a close, we were departing Venice, walking past the two large columns in St. Mark's Square, when all at once I was crushed by my own ton of bricks. A tidal wave of emotions suddenly swept me away, and I burst uncontrollably into tears, crying loudly, right there in the populated square, unconcerned as to the spectacle I was creating. Now, I am a mature woman, and I had known all along when we would have to leave, which is why my reaction was so unforeseen and irrational. Why was I reacting this way? What was wrong with me? All I knew was that it felt like the cruel practicalities of time and our schedule were heartlessly tearing me away, against my will. I felt the desperate need to reach out for control and stability. The bewildering truth was gradually dawning on me that I was exquisitely and intensely in the throes of a new passionate love.

Leaving seemed unbearable, so I dug my proverbial heels into the cobblestones; I just had to stay, at least for a while. I found a place to sit and just lingered for what must have been hours, (time is of no consequence when you are falling in love), breathing in that damp, musky scent that is unique to Venice, trying to somehow absorb her essence into my being and immerse myself in her. After some time, exhausted of snot and tears and of helplessly trying to soak up and retain some trace of her, practicality took over, and I collected myself, still convulsing with sobs, and said goodbye. I walked drearily to the *vaporetto* and watched the dim lights of Venice blur into the mist as we chugged away. I was already suffering acute separation anxiety and was intensely fearful that I would never see her again.

Back at home during the next few years, my personal life proceeded to become much more complicated and financially restricted, and it seemed increasingly less likely that I would ever be able to go back to Venice again. But my longing to return only grew stronger and stronger. I felt drawn by invisible ropes; I just had to find a way to get back to Venice. So I did what any woman in love would do—I found a way to return!

I made my first pilgrimage back alone a couple of years later and was reunited with my love. Her beauty was even more exquisite than I remembered, and my joy was complete as I again walked her cobblestoned streets and immersed myself in her essence, relishing her delights. It was then that something unexpected occurred; a transformation took place; that was when I became A Beautiful Woman in Venice. At first I thought I could get my fill of Venice. But true love never fades, and my love for Venice does not diminish but grows and changes with my increased familiarity. She has become a part of me, has changed me, and her magic continues to inspire me.

Biography

Vonda has traveled several times a year to Venice since 2006 when she fell in love with the city. At home she owns and operates a gift shop in New York where she sells many items including Murano Glass pieces. She collaborated together with Kathleen González on her A Beautiful Woman in Venice *project, which tells the stories of many historical Venetian women who did positive and remarkable things. Kathleen authored the book, and Vonda organizes groups of women to travel to Venice and to visit sites related to these women.*

Website: abeautifulwomaninvenice.com

Facebook: facebook.com/abeautifulwomaninvenice

"*Mia Venezia, Mia Serenissima*: A Boy's First Love" by Marco Zecchin

We ran for our lives, as the angry street vendor from *traghetto Molo* chased us. My brother and I stayed close behind our cousins, running full tilt, past the Palazzo Ducale. Up the Ponte della Paglia, we dodged tourists oohing and taking photographs of the iconic Ponte dei Sospiri. The middle-aged vendor pulled up at the foot of the bridge panting Venetian curses, identifying us as *delinquenti*, alarming everyone who heard his breathless cries. There were other curses that my twelve-year-old ears didn't understand, but I didn't slow to find out what they meant. Ahead of us, as we reached the top of the bridge, the crowds of tourists parted in fear of all the commotion. Cameras, purses, and children were pulled closer to protect them from the four preteen *delinquenti*, effectively clearing the path of our escape.

We slowed a bit reaching the opposite side of the bridge, but in front of the Hotel Danieli we heard the doormen carry the alarm telling us to stop. While they tried to grab us, we each dodged their reach and continued forward running again, afraid they would follow. A few steps were all they took, not straying far from their posts alongside the iconic hotel's entry.

My cousin Giovanni, followed by his brother Pasquale, my brother Peter and I, took a hard left in search of a place to hide. Without hesitation, Giovanni headed straight for sanctuary in Chiesa di San Zaccaria.

Slamming through the church's double doors, we hid crouching between pews.

So how did we get into such a pickle? Well, it started earlier that morning, on the first full day visiting our Venetian family, and to my brother's and my surprise, we were allowed to go out with only our cousins, Venice as our playground. With a stern "*Ti raccomando...*" and a thousand lire each, Pasquale and Giovanni led us through *Venezia's calli e canali.*

On our way, my cousins exchanged "*bon di's*" with vendors they knew and friends they met along the way. They introduced us as their American cousins, and we shared our Italian greetings with them. Most were surprised at our Italian fluency, which made me feel proud and accepted—even at home—in this wonderful and strange city.

Meeting locals meant hearing people speak in the Venetian dialect—a musical dialect that contracts words as often is it drops ending vowels. To that date, I had only heard my father speak in the dialect with other Venetians we met back home in California. It rings nostalgically in my ears whenever I hear it, especially after my father's passing.

The cacophony of cheerful morning greetings being exchanged, hissing espresso machines and overnight shop screens being rolled up, remain as Venetian to me as the midnight bells of San Marco or the gondoliers' "*Oi*" announcement' as they approach canal corners. The smell of coffee and pastries mixed with the salt air has a Pavlovian response in me every time I visit. A day in Venice cannot truly start without a *caffè e brioche*.

A few turns away from my aunt and uncle's front door, we arrived at the Rialto Bridge. Just opening for the day's business were the jewelry, leather, and mask shops. We didn't waste time crossing Rialto, and the smell of tanned leather quickly gave way to the fragrance of fresh fish as we got closer to the Campo della Pescaria—the fish market. My father was born and raised in Venice, so fish was a regular part of our home meals. The Carniglia Brothers' fish market on the municipal pier in Santa Cruz, California, was my parents' favorite. Fresh fish was neatly arranged on beds of ice while either John or Jocko, who remained from the original five Carniglia brothers, prepped my mother's fish selection for the coming week's dinners. But Venice's Pescaria is a spectacle all its own. The Adriatic and Mediterranean Seas grow an amazing array of fish. Tables covered in ice displayed the strange shapes in rainbow colors that accompany the fresh sea and lemon fragrance. Every now and again a whiff of grilled fish would waft by, and even though it was early morning, I wanted to know when we'd be heading home for lunch.

While my cousins placed an order to bring back home for lunch, a writhing tank filled with black eels caught my attention. These delicacies are netted in the canals along the fringe of the Venetian lagoon. A net stretched on long poles across a canal is lowered to the bottom, chummed, and then some time later raised containing the wriggling eels and assorted lagoon fish. As I peered into the tank, there seemed to be no room for water, only the eels sliding around each other with an eye or mouth every now and again coming into view. A customer asked for a couple, which the monger reached in and magically pulled out. In his grasp, they wrapped themselves around his arm before being wrangled into butcher paper and wrapped alive. After this initiation, it would be decades before I'd even try this tasty meal.

From the Campo della Pescaria we took the Traghetto di Santa Sofia. My first "gondola" ride. Well it's not really a gondola but a large gondola-looking boat with rowers at the front and back, a ferry service spanning a section of the Grand Canal with no readily accessible bridge. At that time in the late '60s, this transit was mainly used by locals. When we approached, there were already ten people aboard, and other than a sitting plank near the bow and stern, already taken by a mother and her two children and an elderly couple, we only had standing room. Was it the challenge of my cousins standing or my Venetian heritage bubbling up though my cells, I'll never know, but there was a sense of pride in making my way across standing without stumbling or falling into the canal.

Giving my brother and me a bit of a tour, our cousins wandered around for a couple of hours till we had to get back home for lunch.

The *palazzo* where my aunt and uncle live has been in their family for generations and was as much museum as home. Every wall, corner, and drawer contained paintings, documents, or some artifact from the Venetian Republic, and after lunch we were shown around by my uncle. But it was my uncle's scale models of tall ships that caught my imagination. He was a particular gentleman, allowing us to look but not touch these highly detailed models he hoped would be shown at the Museo Storico Navale di Venezia. Seeing our interest, he showed us how to make a cannon to fit one of his ship models from brass tubing and bits of wood that could fire caps across the room. In a few hours we each had our own miniature cannon that we fired in mock battle for the rest of our visit.

But cannons or not, we were still young boys, and we had to move—if only to buy more caps for the cannons.

Heading in the opposite direction of our morning exploration, our cousins led us through a more claustrophobic series of *sotoportici* and extremely narrow *calli*. Turn after turn, my directional confusion got worse as I followed my newly acquainted cousins anxiously. Eyes on their back, through the river of tourists, I wasn't able to look for visual landmarks to ease my fears in finding my way back if I got separated from them. At what seemed the limit of my ability to keep my fears in check, we came through the arched base of the Torre dell'Orologio–Clock Tower—into the expanse of Piazza San Marco, a spectacle of architectural wonders being revealed in an instant.

I was so affected that I had not realized I was standing still with people complaining and jostling me to move. Yes, I had seen photographs of the *piazza* and the basilica I was named after, but the experience of coming through the archway will forever stop me in my tracks to gawk in awe.

A year earlier I had been introduced to black and white photography by a commercial photographer and high school friend of my mother's. Now, on first glance I thought I'd become color blind in the black and white world of the *piazza*: the sooted marble façade of the *piazza*, gray stone pavement, and white curtains drawn back between the marble colonnade of arches. Yes, there were colored bits of blue sky through clouds, the red brick *campanile*, and mosaic lunettes coloring the face of the *Basilica di San Marco*, but they only accented my perception of this monochrome marvel.

The caffès' live orchestras filled the air with music as I watched the white-jacketed *camerieri* bringing colorful aperitifs to seated tourists taking a respite from their cameras, parcels, and valises. The locals were also obvious; men dressed in their starched white shirts, linen suits, and ties, women in their flowing dresses, colorful scarves, and hats were seated in the immaculately clean white chairs. A simple nod to a familiar *cameriere* was all they needed for their "usual."

A few more colors started to appear as I noticed the vendors with their stalls of trinkets, guidebooks, and seed packets to entice the monochrome pigeons to perch on your hand for photographs—if you were brave enough.

Making our way around the *piazza*, we found our way past the Palazzo Ducale to the gondola-lined quay of the blue-green Bacino di San Marco. With Giovanni in the lead, we followed him to a vendor seated on a low stool. In front of him was a plastic basin filled with canal water and a half dozen windup ducks that paddled and quacked along bumping into each other. There was a crowd of smaller children kneeling and sitting on their heels watching the toy ducks and parents hanging back deciding whether or not to buy one of the toys for their pleading children.

Giovanni had seen this vendor before and was incensed by his subterfuge. In an intentionally loud voice, my nine-year-old cousin explained to us that the quacking was not from the toy ducks but from the hidden "quacker" the vendor had in his mouth. In this revelation, the parents, children, and anyone in earshot fell silent. What followed necessitated our need to run.

There in the sanctuary of Chiesa di San Zaccaria, catching our breath in the marble-cooled air, we tried unsuccessfully to control our nervous giggles. Startled parishioners scowled and shushed us. The *monsignore*, who was tending the altar, came to see what was causing all the commotion. He recognized my cousins and ushered us out and asked what had made us so disrespectful. Giovanni confessed our story to the *monsignore* who knew of the particular vendor. He shook his head and with a quiet curse for the vendor, blessed us, and with another *ti raccomando* we were off waving our *arrivederci*.

Taking a path that kept us away from the villainous vendor, we walked back to the house laughing uncontrollably, each of us retelling the tale of our successful escape from our own perspective and pride in Giovanni's bravery.

In that first day, we cousins forever bonded.

But it was *Venezia*, sharing her *calli e canali*, the intimacy of her morning sounds and fragrances, her iridescent water and marble, her black gondolas elegantly dancing to a watery beat, her beauty and villainy, that created an unbreakable bond, a love, that, with every visit, heals my heart and soul, making me, in each arrival proclaim, "*Mia Venezia, mia Serenissima*."

Biography

Marco was born in America to Italian parents where home was Terra Italiana. *Speaking Italian, eating Italian, driving Italian was his upbringing, helping him appreciate the advantages and challenges of a multicultural life. Traveling regularly to his home and extended family in Italy, he identifies himself as father, owner of Image Center Architectural Photography, fine art photographer, and author of* The Spirit of Northern Italy.

Website: marcozecchin.com
Facebook: Marco Zecchin
Instagram: mzecchin

Acknowledgments

Usually I use this space to thank the people who helped me to bring my own writing to fruition—those who edited, commented, cheered, and brought me drinks. But with *First Spritz Is Free*, I must thank the contributors in a different way. This book exists because they wrote it: They remembered and dreamed, they converted ideas into paragraphs, and they generously sent them all to me to make into this book. Thank you to all these contributors for the hours they spent writing and the talent they shared with me. When I said, "I've got this idea to create a free book. I can't pay you, but will you write something for it?" And every single one of them did.

Thank you as well to the behind the scenes folks, the cheerleaders, listeners, and idea people. Special thanks to Piero Bellini, Adriano Contini, and Marco Zecchin for assisting with the cover design and Iris Loredana for designing the final book cover. Laura Morelli shared her publishing knowledge with me and offered advice on ebook formats, cover art, marketing, and more, for which I am very grateful. Thanks to Jeni Lucas who helped out with legal language. I also appreciated translation help from Tiziana Businaro and Gregory Dowling. Thanks, too, to JoAnn Locktov, Michelle Lovric, Gregory Dowling, Piero Bellini, and Barbara Lynn-Davis who put me in touch with other contributors, expanding my Venetophile community.

Every day I think of how grateful I am to have RJ Wofford II in my life as my partner, and not only because he helps me create every book I've written. But he deserves thanks for that, too.

If you've enjoyed this book and would like to do something to protect and preserve Venice's unique art, architecture, and heritage, please consider contributing to the following organizations:

Savevenice.org
Veniceinperil.org
nograndinavi.it

CPSIA information can be obtained
at www.ICGtesting.com
Printed in the USA
BVHW040614211120
593833BV00026B/705

9 781724 304735